ART MASTERS

THE ART OF THE
RENAISSANCE

LUCIA CORRAIN

ILLUSTRATED BY
L. R. GALANTE & SIMONE BONI

THE OLIVER PRESS, INC.
MINNEAPOLIS

Produced by
DoGi, Firenze
Original title
L'Europa del Rinascimento
Text
Lucia Corrain
Illustrations
L.R. Galante
Simone Boni
Visualization
Sergio
Picture research
Katherine Forden
Graphic design
Oliviero Ciriaci
Art direction and page design
Sebastiano Ranchetti
Editing
Andrea Bachini
Renzo Rossi
English translation
Susan Ashley
Editor, English-language edition
Susan Ashley
Cover design
Icon Productions

© 1997 DoGi s.r.l.
Florence, Italy

First Italian edition
© June 1997 by
L'Airone di Giorgio Mondadori
e Associati s.p.a.
Via Andrea Ponti 8/10
20143 Milano, Italia

© 2008 by VoLo publisher srl,
Firenze, Italia

This edition © 2008 by
The Oliver Press, Inc.
5707 West 36th Street
Minneapolis, MN 55416
United States of America
www.oliverpress.com

Publisher Cataloging Information

Corrain, Lucia
        The art of the Renaissance / Lucia
Corrain ; illustrated by L. R. Galante &
Simone Boni ; [English translation, Susan
Ashley].
        p. cm. – (Art masters)
        Includes bibliographical
references and index.
        Summary: This book is an
illustrated survey of the art and culture of
Renaissance Europe, a period in European
history spanning the fifteenth and sixteenth
centuries.
        ISBN 978-1-934545-04-1
        1. Art, Renaissance–Juvenile
literature   [1. Art, Renaissance   2. Art
appreciation]   I. Galante, L. R.
II. Boni, Simone   III. Ashley, Susan
IV. Title   V. Series
        2008
        709'.02'4–dc22

ISBN 978-1-934545-04-1
Printed in Italy
11 10 09 08   4 3 2 1

♦ HOW TO USE THIS BOOK

Each double-page spread is a chapter in its own right, devoted to a particular place that was important in the Renaissance period or to a type of art characteristic of the time. The theme of each spread is introduced in the main paragraph at the top of the left-hand page (1) and depicted in the large, central illustration. The left-hand column provides historical context, while the smaller text and illustrations on each spread expand on the central theme.

1

Some pages are devoted to major artists of the Renaissance period. The text in the left-hand column (1) provides biographical information, while the large paragraph at the top of the page gives an overview of their artistic style and the techniques they introduced. The spread is illustrated with important works by each artist.

1

CONTENTS

CONTEMPORARIES

The Renaissance is a period in European history spanning the fifteenth and sixteenth centuries. It was an extraordinary era, marked by advances in nearly every sphere of human endeavor, including science, exploration, philosophy, literature, and, most notably, the visual arts. A profusion of supremely gifted artists, including Leonardo da Vinci, Michelangelo, Brunelleschi, Jan van Eyck, and El Greco, emerged during this period to create some of the world's greatest masterpieces in architecture, sculpture, and painting. The Renaissance was a time of remarkable rulers as well. Their patronage stimulated the enormous creative output of the period. The Renaissance began in the city of Florence, in northern Italy, at the beginning of the fifteenth century. It gradually spread to the rest of Europe and reached its full expression in the sixteenth century.

✦TURA AND MANTEGNA
Two great northern Italian painters from the fifteenth century. Tura is associated with the city of Ferrara, while Mantegna was court painter in Mantua.

✦GRÜNEWALD, CRANACH, AND DÜRER
The three leading Renaissance artists in Germany. Their works were often intensely emotional. Albrecht Dürer, the most well-known German Renaissance painter, was also a skilled engraver.

✦EL GRECO
Spanish painter of the sixteenth century, noted for the haunting spirituality of his works and his dramatic use of color.

✦FEDERICO AND LORENZO
Masters of Urbino and Florence in the fifteenth century, these were two enlightened rulers of flourishing Renaissance courts.

✦MASACCIO AND PIERO DELLA FRANCESCA
Two artists who pioneered the technique of perspective and brought a new realism to Early Renaissance painting.

✦VAN EYCK AND BRUEGEL
Flemish painters of the fifteenth and sixteenth centuries whose art was notable for its realism and meticulous attention to detail.

✦ QUEEN ISABELLA OF CASTILE
She was instrumental in uniting the Kingdom of Spain and setting it on a course to become the dominant power in Europe.

ISABELLA D'ESTE ✦
Under her patronage, great artists, writers, and scholars gathered at the court of Mantua, making it a brilliant center of Renaissance culture.

♦ FRANCIS I AND CHARLES V
The king of France and his rival, the Holy Roman Emperor. Their courts were centers of art and learning during the first half of the sixteenth century.

♦ TITIAN AND GIOVANNI BELLINI
Venetian Renaissance painting originated in the fifteenth century with Giovanni Bellini and culminated in the sixteenth century with Titian.

♦ FOUQUET AND COUSIN THE ELDER
French Renaissance artists, Fouquet was the most celebrated French painter of the fifteenth century, while Cousin was an eminent artist of the sixteenth.

♦ RAPHAEL AND DA VINCI
Two giants of Renaissance art. Raphael was admired for his paintings of unsurpassed beauty and harmony. Da Vinci excelled in all of the arts and sciences.

PHILIP II ♦
King of Spain for over forty years (1556–1598), and heir to a large part of Charles V's empire, Philip was a zealous champion of the Catholic Church and patron of the arts.

BRUNELLESCHI ♦ AND DONATELLO
Architect and sculptor. Inspired by classical art, they made Florence the first great center of Renaissance art.

♦ HOLBEIN AND HENRY VIII
Holbein, a German painter, moved to England, where he became the official court portrait painter to King Henry VIII, the monarch who broke away from the Catholic Church.

♦ MICHELANGELO AND JULIUS II
While working for Pope Julius II in Rome, Michelangelo created some of the greatest masterpieces of High Renaissance art, including the painting of the Sistine Chapel ceiling.

RENAISSANCE EUROPE

Raphael, portrait of Leonardo da Vinci, detail from *The School of Athens,* c. 1510, Stanza della Segnatura, Vatican, Rome.

Between 1347 and 1350, a plague known as the Black Death devasted Europe, killing over a third of the continent's population and leading to widespread economic depression. By the end of the fifteenth century, the population had recovered and there was renewed demand for goods and services. This stimulated business and trade, particularly in the wealthy city-states on the Italian peninsula. Italian merchant ships carried goods, as well as Renaissance ideas, to the rest of Europe. Advances in printing technology and intermarriage between members of European royal families spread Renaissance concepts even further. Diplomacy also contributed to a regular exhange of ideas as rulers sent resident ambassadors to courts throughout Europe.

✦ THE SPREAD OF IDEAS

Renaissance art and ideas spread throughout Europe in a variety of ways. The Renaissance saw the birth of modern diplomacy, with rulers sending resident ambassadors to foreign courts to represent them. With the revival of trade in the fifteenth century, Italian merchants and bankers moved to foreign cities, bringing Italian art with them and bringing local art back to Italy. Often, the artists themselves traveled. There was competition among Renaissance rulers to have the most beautiful palaces, churches, and public buildings, and they could afford to hire the most talented artists to create them. King Francis I brought Leonardo da Vinci all the way to France in the sixteenth century, and German artist Hans Holbein traveled to England, where he worked for Henry VIII. Sometimes artists followed patrons who moved to new courts because of marriage. In this way, Renaissance styles and techniques gradually spread throughout Europe as artists came into contact with each other's work.

✦ MUSICIANS
The musicians are dressed in costumes inspired by Greek mythology. The statue at the top represents Apollo, the Greek god of light, healing, and the arts, especially music.

✦ THE OCCASION
In 1573, in the gardens of the new royal palace in Paris, Polish ambassadors offer the crown of Poland to Henry of Valois, brother of Charles IX, the king of France.

✦ AMBASSADORS
Representatives of the Venetian Republic and Russia meet with envoys of the Ottoman Empire at the French court.

HENRY OF VALOIS ✦
(1551–1589) In 1574, less than a year after his coronation as king of Poland, Henry returned to France to succeed his brother Charles IX on the throne. He became King Henry III of France.

THE DELEGATION ✦
The visiting Polish delegation, in traditional costume, mingles with members of the elegant Parisian court.

CATHERINE ✦ DE MEDICI
(1519–1589) Wife of King Henry II of France and Florentine by birth, she helped to establish Italian Renaissance culture at the French court. Henry of Valois was her favorite son.

CHARLES IX ✦
(1550–1574)
The second son of Catherine de Medici. He came to the throne at the age of ten and was dominated by his mother throughout his reign.

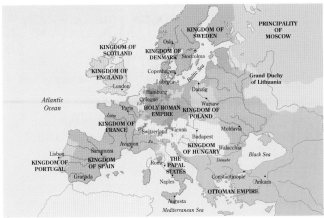

✦EUROPE
At the end of the fifteenth century, the Italian peninsula and the Holy Roman Empire were comprised of independent states and territories. Spain had only recently become a unified kingdom.

✦PAOLO UCCELLO
Battle of San Romano, 1456, tempera on panel, 6 ft. x 10 ft. 5 in. (182 x 317 cm), National Gallery, London.

✦HANS HOLBEIN, THE YOUNGER
The Ambassadors, 1533, tempera on panel, 81.5 x 82.25 in. (207 x 209 cm), National Gallery, London.

✦VITTORE CARPACCIO
Arrival of the Ambassadors of Britain at the Court of Brittany, 1495–1496, tempera on panel, 9 ft. x 19 ft. 4 in. (275 x 589 cm), Accademia, Venice.

THE REVIVAL OF ANTIQUITY

The Renaissance began in Italy in the fifteenth century. It was inspired by the rediscovery of sculpture, architecture, and literature from ancient Greece and Rome. Forgotten or lost during the Middle Ages, classical texts made their way to Italy through merchant ships and the arrival of scholars fleeing Constantinople after its capture by the Ottoman Turks in 1453. In Rome, the physical remains of ancient Rome were scattered throughout the city and rediscovered during excavations. These events sparked a new enthusiasm for art and learning throughout Italy. The revival of interest in antiquity is at the heart of the Renaissance. In fact, the word "Renaissance" means "rebirth" in French. It refers to the rebirth of art and ideas from the classical world.

✦ **RESCUING A WORK OF ART**
During excavations in Rome, the capital, or top, of a column is being cleaned. It is part of the remains of the Temple of Concord, originally built in the fourth century B.C. and rebuilt in the first century A.D. The capital is almost intact. Workers are measuring it and taking note of its proportions. The capital's ornate style is called "Corinthian" and originated in ancient Greece.

✦ **ITALIAN STATES**
Italy in the fifteenth century was comprised of independent city-states. The most powerful were the Duchy of Milan, the Republic of Venice, the Republic of Florence, the Papal States, and the Kingdom of Naples. Urbino, Ferrara, and Mantua were smaller city-states.

LEARNING FROM THE RUINS ✦
Renaissance artists were drawn to Rome because of its abundance of ancient ruins. Architects studied them to understand the methods of Roman builders, while scholars identified and recorded the major sites.

♦ RUINS
This stately row of columns formed part of an ancient Roman temple.

APOLLO ♦
Apollo, Second century A.D. (Vatican, Rome). Renaissance artists were inspired by classical works of art discovered in Rome. The ancient Greeks and Romans regarded the human body as the ultimate expression of perfection.

♦ FROM TEMPLE TO CHURCH
This ancient columned temple was converted into a Christian church.

♦ PRESERVING THE PAST
Architects often incorporated the stones of ancient buildings and the ruins of Roman monuments, like the huge vaults of the Basilica of Maxentius, in their new structures.

Domenico Ghirlandaio, portrait of Marsilio Ficino, detail from *Angel Appearing to Zacharias*, 1490, fresco, Tornabuoni Chapel, Santa Maria Novella, Florence.

♦ HUMANISM
The rediscovery of ancient texts led to the birth of an intellectual movement known as Humanism. Humanism stressed the dignity of man and celebrated human achievement. The movement inspired scholars, writers, and artists throughout the Renaissance. For scholars, it fostered the study of classical literature, history, poetry, philosophy, and science. For artists, it stimulated attempts to represent the physical world using the principles of harmony and balance found in classical art. In painting, this led to important discoveries in perspective and proportion. In both sculpture and painting, the human form took on new significance. Figures became more realistic and portrait painting reached new heights. Inspired by Humanism's confidence in human thought and creativity, many Renaissance artists practiced multiple disciplines. Da Vinci, for example, was a painter, sculptor, architect, engineer, and mathematician.

FLORENCE

Florence is the cradle of the Renaissance. The innovations in art and literature that spread throughout Europe began in this northern Italian republic. The Florentine artist Giotto painted the city's first masterpieces in the late thirteenth century. The flowering of Renaissance ideas, however, began in the fifteenth century when the city was led by the powerful Medici family. Under the patronage of Cosimo the Elder and later his grandson, Lorenzo the Magnificent, the city became a glittering center of art and culture. The most talented artists and architects lived in Florence, and its wealthy merchants financed large-scale projects for them, including the city's splendid new cathedral.

Above: a gold florin, with a lily — the symbol of Florence.

♦ THE CITY

Florence was founded in Roman times, but it wasn't until the eleventh century that the city began to prosper. At the beginning of the fourteenth century, its population had grown to over 50,000, making it one of the most populous cities in Europe. By the fifteenth century, Florence was flourishing. Textiles and banking were the foundation of its wealth. The gold florin of Florence, first minted in 1252, was the standard currency of trade all over Europe. The Medicis were Florence's leading family during the Renaissance. They were also the leaders of Europe's largest bank. They could afford to commission large projects. In addition to the Medicis, powerful merchant guilds played an active role in the city's economic and political life.

Below: A portrait of a Medici by Jacopo Pontormo: *Cosimo the Elder,* c. 1518, detail, oil on panel, Uffizi, Florence.

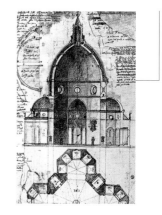

♦ THE DOME
The double-walled dome measures 141 feet (43 m) in diameter. It is slightly smaller than the dome of the Pantheon in Rome, which was the largest dome in the ancient world. Section of the Florence Cathedral dome, drawing, c. 1440.

MARBLE ♦
Workers unload a block of marble from an ox-drawn cart. Pulleys are used to raise the heavy stone and move it. Panels of colored marble cover the outside of the cathedral, and white marble forms the ribs of the dome.

♦ FLORENCE CATHEDRAL
Work on the cathedral began in 1296. Between 1334 and 1337, the artist Giotto oversaw the project and designed the belltower. Work proceeded slowly during the fourteenth century and ended in 1436 with the completion of Brunelleschi's great dome. The cathedral was the largest in Europe and could hold 10,000 people.

MATERIALS ♦
A finished block of white marble that will be used for a rib in the high part of the dome.

♦ BRUNELLESCHI'S DOME
Filippo Brunelleschi won a competition to design the cathedral's dome. It took sixteen years to build. Over four million bricks were used in its construction. Brunelleschi's design allowed it to be built without the use of scaffolding.

♦ VIEW
A view of Renaissance Florence and its majestic cathedral.

♦ THE BUILDING SITE
A high fence marks the boundary of the building site. Dozens of laborers, including stonemasons, carpenters, blacksmiths, and mechanics, are at work, divided into teams under the leadership of a master builder.

MACHINES ♦
In addition to designing the dome, Brunelleschi designed many of the machines used to construct it.

ROPES ♦
Two laborers carry a heavy length of rope on their backs, sharing its weight between them. Ropes were vital for transmitting the muscle power of humans or animals to machines to make them work.

Filippo Brunelleschi, Pazzi Chapel, 1430, Church of Santa Croce, Florence.

♦ FILIPPO BRUNELLESCHI
(1377–1446)
Brunelleschi's major works were built in the city of Florence. In addition to the cathedral dome, he designed the churches of San Lorenzo and Santo Spirito, the Foundling Hospital, and the Pazzi Chapel (above). He was fascinated by math and engineering, and designed machines for construction as well as for use in theatrical productions.

Piero della Francesca, *Annunciation,* 1470, oil and tempera on panel, 48 x 76.5 in. (122 x 194 cm), Galleria Nazionale dell'Umbria, Perugia.

♦ PERSPECTIVE
Artists use perspective to make images on a flat surface appear as if they are three-dimensional, or to create the illusion of distance between objects. Brunelleschi made the first known perspective drawing around 1415. He discovered that if the outlines of buildings or objects are extended, they converge on a vanishing point. Many Italian artists adopted this method of creating perspective.

FLORENTINE SCULPTURE

Above and below:
Sacrifice of Isaac,
bronze reliefs for the
Baptistry door, 1401,
by Lorenzo Ghiberti
(above) and Filippo
Brunelleschi
(below), Bargello
Museum, Florence.

✦ THE BAPTISTRY

In 1401, Florence
held a famous
competition to select
a designer for the
north doors of the
Florence Cathedral
Baptistry. Entrants
had to make a
bronze panel
portraying the
sacrifice of Isaac.
The competition was
ultimately narrowed
to two men: Lorenzo
Ghiberti and Filippo
Brunelleschi. The
entire city was divid-
ed between the two
artists. In the end,
Ghiberti was
selected. He was
only twenty-three
years old. It took
him twenty-one
years to complete
the doors, which
consist of twenty-
eight bronze panels.
The doors brought
fame to Ghiberti and
he received many
new commissions,
including the design
of the east doors of
the Baptistry. He
finished the east
doors just three
years before his
death. Michelangelo
claimed they were fit
to be the "Gates of
Paradise."

Florence was the wealthiest city in Europe at the beginning of the fifteenth century. It sought to express its wealth through grand artistic projects. One of these was the decoration of Orsanmichele (or sahn mee kay lay), an important building in the city. Orsanmichele was a grain market that had been converted into a church, with fourteen niches, or recesses, in its outer walls. City guilds were assigned to place statues of their patron saints in each of the niches. The guilds were made up of owners and managers of the city's businesses. They were proud groups and each tried to outdo the other in the decoration of its niche. Orsanmichele became a showcase of Florentine sculpture. It featured the work of Donatello, Lorenzo Ghiberti, and Nanni di Banco, whose realistic sculpture represented the new language of the Renaissance.

✦ SAINT GEORGE

This statue was
commissioned by
the armorers' guild
of Florence. The
figure of St. George
shows a naturalism
that contrasts with
the stiff figures of
Gothic sculpture,
which preceded the
Renaissance.
Donatello,
St. George,
1415–1416, marble,
height 6 ft. 5 in.
(378 cm), Bargello
Museum, Florence.

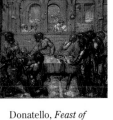

Donatello, *Feast of Herod*, 1427, bronze relief for baptismal font, Baptistry, Siena.

♦ ST. JOHN THE BAPTIST
Lorenzo Ghiberti, *St. John the Baptist*, 1412–1416, bronze, height 8 ft. 4 in. (254 cm), Orsanmichele, Florence.

♦ DONATELLO
Donato di Niccolò di Betto Bardi, better known as Donatello (c. 1386–1466), began his artistic career as one of Ghiberti's assistants on the north door of the Florentine Baptistry. He became skilled in bronze working with Ghiberti. From Brunelleschi, with whom he spent time in Rome studying ancient ruins, he learned the principles of perspective, which he brilliantly applied to his work. Donatello had close ties to Cosimo de Medici, who brought him work. The expressive quality of his sculpture was an inspiration to other Italian artists, in particular, Mantegna and Bellini.

Ghiberti, detail from *St. Matthew*.

♦ ORSANMICHELE
The monumental figures made for the outside walls of Orsanmichele between 1410 and 1428 were the first important Renaissance sculptures. Inspired by classical statues, they exhibited a sense of realism that had been missing from art for centuries.

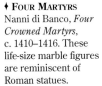

♦ FOUR MARTYRS
Nanni di Banco, *Four Crowned Martyrs*, c. 1410–1416. These life-size marble figures are reminiscent of Roman statues.

♦ ST. MATTHEW
Lorenzo Ghiberti, *St. Matthew*, 1419–1422, bronze, height 8 ft. 10 in. (270 cm), Orsanmichele, Florence.

♦ LORENZO GHIBERTI
Ghiberti (1378–1455) was a sculptor, goldsmith, architect, painter, and writer. He desgined the famous Baptistry doors. When the bankers' guild hired him to design St. Matthew for Orsanmichele, they demanded it be as grand as the niche he had designed for the wool merchants' guild.

MASACCIO

The realistic style mastered by Florentine sculptors of the Early Renaissance soon found an equivalent in the paintings of another Florentine, the youthful Masaccio (mah sah choh). In his famous fresco cycle in the Brancacci Chapel in Florence, he created lifelike human figures within what appeared to be real space. In another fresco, *The Trinity*, he made striking use of the new rules of perspective. Masaccio introduced a simplicity and naturalism to painting that was unknown in the Middle Ages. His use of lighting and perspective gave his paintings a realism that greatly influenced other Italian masters. Masaccio was only in his twenties when he died, yet his pictorial innovations made him the first master of Renaissance painting.

Self-portrait of Masaccio. Detail from *The Raising of the Son of Theophilus*, 1427–1428, fresco, 90.5 in. x 19 ft. 7.5 in. (230 x 598 cm), Brancacci Chapel, Santa Maria del Carmine, Florence.

✦ MASACCIO
Tommaso Cassai, known as Masaccio, was born near Florence in 1401. He showed great artistic talent at an early age and began his brief working career in 1422. In 1425, he was commissioned by a wealthy Florentine merchant, Felice Brancacci, to paint a series of frescoes in a chapel of the church of Santa Maria del Carmine in Florence. The frescoes narrate the life of St. Peter. Masaccio received other commissions while working on the chapel, and the frescoes remained unfinished when he died. More than fifty years later, they were completed by Filippino Lippi (1457–1504), who was a pupil of Botticelli, another Florentine painter. Masaccio learned the rules of perspective from the architect Brunelleschi. His naturalistic, three-dimensional figures were inspired by another contemporary, the Florentine sculptor Donatello. Masaccio spent most of his working life in Florence, but died in Rome, where he was working on a commission, in 1428. He was only twenty-seven years old.

✦ THE TRINITY
In this painting, Masaccio used perspective to create an illusion of depth. The chapel's barrel-vaulted ceiling recedes behind the figures in the foreground so that the space represented actually looks like a niche carved into the wall of the church.
Masaccio, *The Trinity*, 1426–1428, fresco, 21 ft. x 10 ft. 5 in (667 x 317 cm), Church of Santa Maria Novella, Florence.

✦ THE BRANCACCI CHAPEL FRESCOES
The fresco cycle begins with *Adam and Eve Tempted by the Serpent* and the subsequent *Expulsion,* (left) 1425, 7 ft. x 2 ft. 11 in. (214 x 90 cm). These frescoes had a profound impact on Michelangelo. Above (whole) and right (detail): *The Tribute Money*, 1425, 8 ft. 1 in. x 19 ft. 7 in. (247 x 597 cm). In the center, Jesus tells Peter where to find the money; on the left, Peter takes the money from a fish's mouth; on the right, Peter hands the money to the tax collector.

✦ ST. PETER BAPTIZES THE NEOPHYTES

The structure of the painting is simple and well balanced. St. Peter and the kneeling man in the foreground are surrounded by a semi-circle of figures. The people in the painting and the mountains in the background are depicted with a realism that was rare at the time.
Left (whole) and detail (right):
St. Peter Baptizing the Neophytes,
1424–1425,
8 ft. 1 in. x 5 ft. 8 in.
(247 x 172 cm).

✦ ST. PETER DISTRIBUTES ALMS TO THE POOR

Here, St. Peter is distributing alms to the poor. Ananias has been reproached for holding back part of his goods and is struck down. The other central figure, a woman holding a child (right), shows Masaccio's skill in depicting human emotion.
Left (whole) and detail (right):
The Distribution of the Goods and the Death of Ananias,
1426–1427,
7 ft. 7 in x 5 ft. 2 in.
(232 x 157 cm).

✦ ST. PETER HEALS A GROUP OF MEN

This story follows that of Ananias in the Acts of the Apostles. Peter walks along a street casting his shadow over a group of crippled men. Masaccio's use of perspective adds depth to the buildings along the street and enhances the sense of movement.
Left (whole) and detail (right):
St. Peter Healing with His Shadow,
1426–1427,
7 ft. 7 in. x 5 ft. 4 in.
(232 x 162 cm).

THE SUPREMACY OF LINE

Masaccio had an enormous impact on fifteenth-century Florentine artists. Many later painters, including Fra Angelico, Filippo Lippi, Ghirlandaio, Botticelli, and Filippino Lippi, studied his work and used it as the basis from which to create their own experiments with light, color, perspective, and composition. These artists also shared a belief in the importance of line. The use of drawn outlines in painting was considered fundamental in giving a solid, sculptural quality to forms and creating a more exact representation of reality. Renaissance painters sought to give their paintings a feeling of depth and their figures individuality and emotion.

LIPPI AND CASTAGNO
Filippo Lippi sought to attain a refined beauty in his art, while Andrea del Castagno aimed for realistic details and human expression.
1. Filippo Lippi, *Madonna and Child with the Birth of the Virgin,* 1452, panel, diameter 53 in. (135 cm), Pitti Palace, Florence.
2. Andrea del Castagno, *Last Supper,* 1447, fresco, 15 ft. 5 in. x 32 ft. (470 x 975 cm), Convent of Santa Apollonia, Florence.

THE MASTERS
Leonardo da Vinci began painting in Verrocchio's workshop and the young Michelangelo studied with Ghirlandaio.
1. Andrea del Verrocchio, *Head of St. Jerome,* c. 1460, tempera on paper, 19.5 x 18 in. (49 x 46 cm), Pitti Palace, Florence.
2. Domenico Ghirlandaio, *Miracle of the French Notary's Child,* 1480, fresco, Santa Trinita Church, Sassetti, Chapel, Florence.

♦ GEOMETRIC ACCURACY
The receding columns and arches create the illusion of depth. Fra Angelico also used light and shading to give the architecture a three-dimensional quality. Fra Angelico, *Annunciation, c.* 1438, fresco, 7 ft. x 10 ft. 6 in. (230 x 321 cm), Monastery of San Marco, Florence.

♦ DEVOTION
Fra Angelico, (c. 1400–1455), worked as an artist in the service of the Dominicans, a religious order founded by St. Dominic. This painting exemplifies the artist's religious devotion, as well as the simple, serene quality of his paintings. Fra Angelico, *St. Dominic at the Foot of the Cross,* 1442, fresco, 7 ft. 9 in x 4 ft. (237 x 125 cm), Monastery of San Marco, Florence.

BOTTICELLI AND LIPPI ♦
Botticelli's art was sensitive and poetic and he enjoyed a close relationship with the Medici family. His *Birth of Venus* depicts the ancient Roman goddess of love and beauty. Filippino Lippi, the son of Filippo Lippi, studied under Botticelli, but his style is less subtle and more detailed than Botticelli's.
1. Filippino Lippi, *Adoration of the Magi* 1496, oil on panel, 8 ft. 5 in. x 8 ft. (258 x 243 cm), Uffizi, Florence.
2. Sandro Botticelli, *Birth of Venus,* c. 1483–1485, tempera on canvas, 5 ft. 9 in. x 9 ft. 2 in. (172 x 278 cm), Uffizi, Florence.

2

Antonio Pollaiolo, *St. Sebastian*, 1475, tempera on panel, 9 ft. 7 in. x 6 ft. 8 in. (292 x 203 cm), National Gallery, London.

2

♦ **FLORENTINE ARTISTS OF THE FIFTEENTH CENTURY**
The Florentine artists of the Early Renaissance were directly influenced by the innovative style of Donatello and Masaccio.
• Filippo Lippi was born in Florence in 1406 and died in Spoleto, a town in central Itay in 1469.
• Andrea del Castagno was born in Tuscany around 1423 and died in Florence in 1457.
• Antonio Pollaiuolo was born in Florence in 1431 and died in Rome in 1498. He was a master of showing the human figure in motion.
• Andrea del Verrocchio was born in Florence in 1435 and died in Venice in 1488. He was a goldsmith, sculptor, and painter.
• Sandro Botticelli, the creator of an exquisite and unique style of painting, was born in Florence in 1445 and died there in 1510.
• Domenico Ghirlandaio was born in Florence in 1449 and died in 1494. He was one of the greatest pictorial chroniclers of the age.
• Filippino Lippi, son of Filippo Lippi, was born in Tuscany in 1457 and died in 1504.

2

LIGHT

Domenico Veneziano, detail of St. John.

Florentine painters in the fifteenth century discovered that using gradations of color was an effective way to represent light. The St. Lucy altarpiece in Florence, painted by Domenico Veneziano in 1445, provides the best illustration of the technique. In this work, Veneziano also reveals the advances made in the use of perspective to produce an illusion of depth. His mastery of light, color, and perspective influenced Piero della Francesa, one of the giants of Renaissance art.

♦ **ANNUNCIATION**
Domenico Veneziano, *Annunciation*. Veneziano's skilled use of perspective gives depth to the graceful colonnaded court leading into the flowered garden.

♦ **THE ST. LUCY ALTARPIECE**
Time and circumstances have scattered many works of art that originally belonged together. This is the case with the St. Lucy altarpiece (1445–1447) whose six parts are now housed in four different museums. The St. Lucy altarpiece was created for the small church of Santa Lucia dei Magnoli in Florence. It depicts the Virgin Mary flanked by four saints.
1. *Madonna and Child with St. Francis, St. John the Baptist, St. Zenobius, and St. Lucy*; tempera on panel, 82 x 84 in. (209 x 216 cm, Uffizi, Florence.
2. *St. Francis Receives the Stigmata*; tempera on panel, 10.5 x 12 in. (26.7 x 30.5 cm), National Gallery of Art, Washington, D.C., Kress Collection.
3. *St. John the Baptist in the Desert*; tempera on panel 11.1 x 12.75 in. (28.3 x 32.4 cm), National Gallery of Art, Washington, D.C., Kress Collection.
4. *Annunciation*; tempera on panel, 10.75 x 21.25 in. (27.3 x 54 cm), Fitzwilliam Museum, Cambridge, England.
5. *Miracle of St. Zenobius*; tempera on panel, 11.25 x 12.75 in. (28.6 x 32.5 cm), Fitzwilliam Museum, Cambridge, England.
6. *Martyrdom of St. Lucy*; tempera on panel, 9.8 x 11.25 in. (25 x 28.5 cm), Gemäldegalerie, Berlin.

1

2  3  4  5  6

Piero della
Francesca,
Baptism of Christ,
detail.

**♦ PIERO DELLA
FRANCESCA**
Piero della
Francesca was born
in the Tuscan town
of Arezzo between
1414 and 1420.
Piero was a
mathematician as
well as an artist and
wrote several
treatises on math.
His interest in
geometry aided him
in his painting,
particularly in his
experiments with
perspective. Around
1435, he became an
apprentice of
Domenico
Veneziano in
Florence. One of his
most celebrated
achievements is the
*Legend of the True
Cross*, a cycle of
frescoes he
completed in 1459
for the church of
San Francesco in
Arezzo. The
frescoes are
examples of his
command of
perspective and
color. Despite
commissions that
took him to several
Italian cities, Piero
spent most of his
life in his native
town, where he
died in 1492. His
absence from
glittering Italian
courts accounts
for the modest
appraisal he
received upon his
death. His influence
on fellow artists,
however, was
considerable.
Today, some art
historians regard
him as the greatest
Italian painter of the
fifteenth century.

♦ LIGHT
In this painting, the figures are lit from above
and are bathed in light. The figure of Christ is
especially luminous. With subtle shading,
however, the artist has given the figure a
solid, sculptural quality.
Piero della Francesca, *Baptism of Christ*
1448–1454, tempera on panel, 66 x 45.75 in.
(167 x 116 cm), National Gallery, London.

♦ LEARNING FROM THE MASTER
The balanced grouping and rich draperies of
the figures' clothing are reminscent of
Domenico Veneziano's work. The vaulted
ceiling is an example of Piero's mastery
of perspective.
Piero della Francesca, *Madonna and Child
with Saints*, 1472–1474, oil on panel, 98 x 79
in. (248 x 170 cm), Brera, Milan.

♦ PERSPECTIVE
According to legend, Paolo Uccello was obsessed with the new science of perspective. In his painting above, the scene
on the left is relatively conventional, with the vanishing point in the center of the back wall. In the scene on the right,
the vanishing point is to the right of the outer wall, putting a bit of strain on the perspective.
Paolo Uccello, *Miracle of the Host,* 1465–1469; tempera on panel, Galleria Nazionale delle Marche, Urbino.

URBINO

The massive Ducal Palace dominates both the skyline and the history of Urbino, a city in central Italy. Erected in the fifteenth century, the palace was built for Federico da Montefeltro, the duke of Urbino. Montefeltro was the personification of a Renaissance lord. He was a brave condottiere (kohn doh tee air ay) — a captain of an army of mercenaries — as well as a man of culture. His enormous palace was considered the finest of its time and he attracted brilliant scholars, painters, architects, and poets to his court. He also assembled one of the largest libraries in Italy. The most important artist to work in Urbino was Piero della Francesca, a mathematician as well as a painter. He made important discoveries regarding the use of perspective in painting.

Above and below: Portraits of Federico da Montefeltro and his wife Battista Sforza, 1465, Uffizi, Florence.

✦ THE CITY

Urbino sits at the top of a hill in a mountainous region in central Italy. The imposing Ducal Palace towers over the surrounding town. The palace was built for Duke Federico da Montefeltro (1422–1482). Work on the palace began in 1454 and was still in progress when the duke died in 1482. Montefeltro had been a professional soldier since the age of sixteen and spent much of his adult life waging war on various Italian city-states, a job for which he was well paid. He was as vigorous off the battlefield as on it, and lost his right eye in a fencing tournament in his late twenties. Thereafter, he insisted that any portraits show only his good side. The portrait below shows the duke in profile, a common portrait style at the time.

✦ THE PALACE CITY

Sitting at the top of a steep cliff, the sprawling Ducal Palace was an awe-inspiring site. It took thirty years to build. The various parts of the complex were carefully built into the existing town, creating an integrated urban design. Baldesar Castiglione, a diplomat and author who lived at the court, described Urbino as being "like a city in the form of a palace."

✦ PIERO DELLA FRANCESCA

The subject of this painting is the flagellation, or whipping, of Jesus by the Romans. There has been much speculation about the identity of the three men in the foreground and why they seem unaffected by the event taking place in the background. While those issues are unresolved, there is no doubt that the painting shows Piero's mastery of perspective. The distance between the two groups of men is realistically portrayed. The painting also displays geometric forms, a sign of Piero's interest in mathematics. *Flagellation*, c. 1460 (whole left and detail below left), oil and tempera on panel, 23.25 x 32.1 in. (59 x 81.5 cm), Galleria Nazionale delle Marche, Palazzo Ducale, Urbino.

FORMAL GARDENS ✦

The duke's wife's quarters overlooked the gardens, which contained a large greenhouse.

THE COURTYARD ✦
Architect Luciano Laurana designed the courtyard, surrounded by elegant arcades. The left wing contains the splended throne room, the largest room in the palace.

✦THE PASQUINO COURTYARD
This wing housed rooms reserved for ambassadors and diplomats. Servants' rooms were at the top.

✦AN IDEAL CITY
In this painting of a fictional, idealized city, a circular building in a classical style is surrounded by a large square and buildings of harmonious proportions.
Ideal City, late fifteenth century, Galleria Nazionale delle Marche, Urbino.

Above and below: The Cathedral and the Town Hall of Pienza.

✦RENAISSANCE CITY
Renaissance architects were inspired by the perfect geometry of classical Greek and Roman buildings. They sought to duplicate their symmetry and harmony in their building designs, and dreamed of planning entire new cities, but lacked the money to carry out such large-scale plans. In Pienza, a small town in Tuscany, however, one man was able to fulfill his vision of a city based on classical ideals. Enea Silvio Piccolomini (1405–1464) was born in Pienza and later became Pope Pius II. As pope, he had the power and influence necessary to put his ideas into action. He rebuilt the small village of Pienza, turning it into a Renaissance town. He added a central piazza, or square, and surrounded it with elegant palaces, a cathedral, and a town hall.

✦THE CORTILE DEL GALLO
The duke's illustrious guests stayed in rooms overlooking this courtyard.

THE GATEHOUSE ✦
Federico's quarters were in the mighty twin-towered gatehouse, over-looking the valley.

✦ THE KEEP
Inside the keep, a wide spiral ramp linked the palace to a plaza outside where markets and parades were held. The low wing next to the keep was a stable large enough to hold over 300 horses.

Above and below:
Cosimo Tura
*Madonna Enthroned
with Musician
Angels*, c. 1480,
details, oil on panel,
94 x 39.75 in. (239 x
101 cm), National
Gallery, London.

✦ THE CITY

Ferrara was situated
between the more
powerful cities of
Milan and Venice,
but under the Este
dukes, it developed
into an important
center of Renais-
sance culture.
During the fifteenth
century, it was ruled
by Niccolò III
(1383–1441), and
later by his three
sons: Lionello
(1407–1450), Borso
(1413–1471), and
Ercole (1431–1505).
Duke Borso put on
lavish spectacles and
spent huge sums of
money on palace
renovations and a
richly illuminated
Bible. When he
rebuilt the Este
summer palace, he
commissioned a
local artist, Cosimo
Tura (c. 1430–1493),
to decorate the
interiors of the
palace with frescoes.
Tura became one of
the founders of the
Ferrara school of
painting. Borso's
brother Ercole was
an enthusiastic
patron of the arts
and the city
flourished under his
rule. Ferrara
became known for
music, as well as
painting and
architecture.

FERRARA

Under the patronage of the powerful Este family,
Ferrara became a leading cultural center during
the fifteenth century. It developed an artistic school
whose painting style was influenced by the painters
Piero della Francesca and Mantegna. Music also
flourished at the court and musicians from all over
Europe came to Ferrara to compose. The Este
dukes lived extravagantly, a way of life that was
characteristic of Italian Renaissance courts. They
attached great importance to displays of courtly
ritual and staged lavish entertainments for the
benefit of visiting dignitaries. These took place at
the magnificent Este palace, in the center of the
city. Many new palaces were built in Ferrara
during the Renaissance, but the city's most
famous structure was its medieval castle
surrounded by a moat.

CLERGYMEN ✦
The presence of
church dignitaries
and representatives
from the Vatican
lends solemnity to
the official
ceremony. Later, the
whole court will
assemble in the
cathedral for Mass.

THE PALACE ✦
The guest rooms in
the Este palace have
been completely
redecorated for the
celebration. They
must be worthy of a
future queen.

THE AMBASSADORS ✦
Ambassadors, or representatives of foreign
rulers, took part in the festivities, wearing the
costumes of their native lands.

♦THE OCCASION
In 1475, the Este court celebrated the visit of Beatrice of Aragon, the sister of Duke Ercole's wife Elenora. Beatrice was on her way to Hungary, where she would wed King Matthias Corvinus. Beatrice contributed to the spread of Italian Renaissance culture in Hungary.

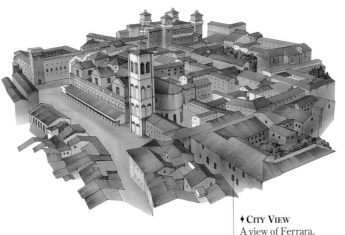

♦ CITY VIEW
A view of Ferrara, the city ruled by the Este family.

THE CASTLE ♦
Symbol of ducal power, the Castle of San Michele was an imposing medieval structure with four defensive towers and surrounded by a moat. It stood next to the Este Palace, to which it was joined for security reasons.

♦THE JOUST
Horsemen prepare to take part in a joust on the parade ground. Jousting, a dangerous sport played on horseback, had been popular since the Middle Ages.

♦ COSIMO TURA
(1430–1493), *Spring*, c. 1460, oil on panel, National Gallery, London.

♦COSIMO TURA
Madonna Enthroned with Musician Angels, 1480, oil, National Gallery, London.

♦OFFICIAL WELCOME
Beneath the ceremonial canopy, Duke Ercole d'Este and his wife Elenora welcome Beatrice, daughter of the King of Naples.

Mantua

Mantua was a small city-state in northern Italy surrounded by a defensive ring of lakes. During the Renaissance, it became one of the most cultured cities in Europe, thanks to the ruling Gonzaga family. The Gonzagas had begun an architectural renovation of the city in the fourteenth century. Ludovico III drove it forward in the fifteenth century with major contributions from the architect Leon Battista Alberti. In 1460, Ludovico appointed Andrea Mantegna court painter of Mantua, a post he would hold for the next forty-six years. Mantegna was one of the most influential Italian painters and his appointment brought great prestige to the city. Mantua continued its role as a center of Renaissance culture under the rule of Ludovico's grandson Francesco and his cultivated wife Isabella d'Este of Ferrara.

Above: Leon Battista Alberti, design for the Church of Sant'Andrea, Mantua, 1472.

♦ ARCHITECTS

The church of Sant'Andrea was a central feature of Mantua's new architectural and urban renewal. The church was the work of Leon Battista Alberti (1404–1472). Alberti had lived in Rome and was very influenced by the ancient ruins there. He used elements of ancient Greek architecture on the facade of Sant'Andrea: a triangular pediment at the top; pilasters, or ornamental columns, rising the entire height of the building; and a colossal arch over the entrance. The church's huge barrel-vaulted interior was copied all over Europe. The architect Giulio Romano (1499–1546) used some of the same features when he designed the Palazzo del Te, a residence for the Gonzaga family in Mantua.

Below: Giulio Romano, detail of a facade of the Palazzo del Te, 1525–1526, Mantua.

♦ THE DUCAL PALACE

The history of the Ducal Palace in Mantua is closely bound up with the Gonzaga family, who held court in the monumental residence between 1328 and 1707. The complex includes several buildings and contains 500 rooms, as well as courtyards and gardens. The Gonzagas hired some of the most talented artists of the time, including Andrea Mantegna and Pisanello, to decorate the palace rooms.

♦ FALCONRY

During the Renaissance, the art of breeding and training birds to hunt was very popular among kings and noblemen.

♦ SEIZE THE PREY!

The lord holds the hooded falcon on his left fist. Beside him rides the falconer, who has trained the bird to hunt. With an upward swing of his arm and a sharp shouted command, the lord launches the bird. The hunting party follows the falcon's swooping flight, guided also by the sound of a bell attached to one of its talons.

24

LA CAMERA ✦ DEGLI SPOSI (THE WEDDING CHAMBER)
This magnificent room in the Ducal Palace is covered from floor to ceiling in frescoes by Mantegna. The frescoes depict scenes from the life of the Gonzaga family.
Right: On the north wall, the family is shown with a group of courtiers and messengers.

✦ DETAILS
Ludovico Gonzaga (left) is recognizable in the scene of the family and court above. Frescoes on the walls of the Camera degli Sposi, 1465–1474, Ducal Palace, Mantua.

Andrea Mantegna, ceiling of the Camera degli Sposi, diameter 8 ft. 10 in. (270 cm), Ducal Palace, Mantua.

✦ MANTEGNA
Andrea Mantegna (1431–1506) is recognized as one of the great masters of Renaissance painting. He was born near Padua, a city northeast of Mantua and close to the city of Venice. He began his artistic apprenticeship with Francesco Squarcione, whose passion for classical antiquities greatly influenced his pupil. He encouraged Mantegna to study Roman sculpture and taught him to speak Latin. In 1453, Mantegna married the daughter of the famous Venetian painter Jacopo Bellini. He worked in Padua and Verona, and in August 1460, entered the court of the Gonzagas in Mantua. Except for brief visits to Florence and Rome, Mantegna spent the next forty-six years in the service of the Gonzagas. It was the longest and most continuous working relationship between an artist and a Renaissance court. In his final years, Mantegna continued painting, despite declining health. He died in Mantua in 1506.

✦THE HUNT
In the countryside beyond Mantua, a hunt with falcons is in progress. Falcons were considered creatures of great nobility. Hunting parties were made up of the lord and his courtiers. They were often accompanied by ladies.

✦THE PACK
Hounds and spaniels retrieve the prey, often squirrels and rabbits. Their trainers reward them with pieces of raw meat.

Above and below:
Bonifacio Bembo,
*Portrait of Francesco
Sforza* and *Portrait of
Bianca Maria Sforza*,
(his wife), 1460,
tempera on canvas,
each 19.25 x 12.25 in.
(49 x 31 cm),
Brera, Milan.

**✦ THE VISCONTI AND
THE SFORZA**
Gian Galeazzo
Visconti (1351–1402)
created the Duchy of
Milan in 1395 and was
its first duke. He
conquered the cities
of Verona, Vicenza,
and Bologna and tried
to seize Florence in an
attempt to unite all of
northern Italy under
one kingdom. In the
fifteenth century, the
Republic of Venice
advanced westward in
its own attempt to
control northern Italy.
Milan and Venice
waged war until 1454,
when a peace treaty
was signed. The
Visconti dynasty
continued under Gian
Galeazzo's two sons.
When the last son
died without an heir,
Francesco Sforza
came to power. The
Sforza dynasty ruled
Milan from 1450 until
1499. Francesco was a
popular ruler who
created a thriving
Renaissance court.
His first son succeed-
ed him, but he was
murdered, leaving
power in the hands of
his seven-year-old son.
The boy passed under
the control of his
uncle, Ludovico
il Moro .

MILAN

During the second half of the fifteenth century,
Milan enjoyed economic prosperity and a cultural
flowering. The court of Ludovico Sforza, known as
"il Moro," was one of the most splendid in Europe.
Ludovico was an enlightened ruler who invited
humanists, painters, and architects to his court.
He commissioned the architect Donato Bramante
to work on the monastery of Santa Maria della
Grazie, where Leonardo da Vinci would paint his
famous *Last Supper* on the wall of the refectory,
or dining hall. Ludovico had scientific as well as
artistic leanings, and the presence of engineers
and mathematicians at his court encouraged
Da Vinci in his own research. In 1499, foreign
invasions led to the fall of Ludovico, the end of
the Sforza dynasty, and the city's decline.

✦ THE LAST SUPPER
One of the most famous paintings in the world,
Da Vinci's *Last Supper* portrays the scene in which
Jesus announces that one of his Disciples will betray
him. The painting is notable for its realism in depict-
ing the Disciples and their reactions to the news.
Leonardo da Vinci, *The Last Supper*, 1495–1497,
tempera on wall, 15 ft. x 29 ft. (460 x 880 cm),
Refectory, Santa Maria delle Grazie, Milan.

✦ SANTA MARIA DELLE GRAZIE
Francesco Sforza ordered the building of a
Dominican convent and church where a small
chapel once stood. The church was completed
during the rule of Ludovico il Moro, who
commissioned Bramante to design the apse
(the end of the church behind the altar), and
Leonardo da Vinci to paint the frescoes.

PERMISSION ✦
Ludovico il Moro
received permission
from the Domincan
monks to modify the
original layout of
Santa Maria della
Grazie and enlarge
the entire complex.

THE THREE ARTISTS ✦
Donato Bramante and
Giovanni Antonio
Amadeo were the
architects who
worked on the build-
ing of Santa Maria
delle Grazie. Here,
they are in discussion
with Da Vinci.

✦ THE LANTERN
The lantern, a gallery at the top of the church with sixteen sides and thirty-two arched bays, is the work of Italian architect and sculptor Giovanni Antonio Amadeo (1447–1522).

✦ THE CLOISTER
The monks lived in this secluded area. The east side of the cloister housed the dormitory where the monks slept. The north side housed a large library of valuable texts.

Above: This cameo, or engraved stone, displays a portrait of Ludovico il Moro. Museo degli Argenti, Florence.

✦ DA VINCI IN MILAN
Lorenzo the Magnificent of Florence sent Leonardo da Vinci to his friend, Ludovico il Moro. Da Vinci arrived in Milan in 1482. With Ludovico's support, he was able to realize his artistic and scientific ambitions. Da Vinci worked in Milan for seventeen years, creating not only paintings, but also architectural plans and monuments. It was also in Milan that Da Vinci made his designs of flying machines. When the Duchy of Milan fell under the control of the French in 1499, Da Vinci returned to Florence.

HIGH RENAISSANCE

The sixteenth century is considered the greatest age of Italian art. The first thirty years or so of the century are called the High Renaissance because they represent the culmination of the artistic knowledge absorbed during the fifteenth century, or the Early Renaissance. Florence was the art capital of the Early Renaissance and, as late as 1504, the three giants of High Renaissance art — Da Vinci, Michelangelo, and Raphael — were all working there. The center of Italian art would soon shift, however, to the city of Rome. Lorenzo the Magnificent, the great Florentine art patron, had died in 1492, and the Medicis were expelled from the city. Stepping in to take their place were a series of ambitious popes who had the power to lure the best artistic talent to Rome.

✦ MONA LISA
Da Vinci set a new standard for the art of portraiture with this painting. It embodies his search for both realism and harmony. Leonardo da Vinci, *Mona Lisa*, 1505–1514, oil on panel, 30.25 x 21 in. (77 x 53 cm), Louvre, Paris.

DAVID ✦
Michelangelo's celebrated statue shows the influence of classical sculpture and represents an ideal of human beauty. Michelangelo, *David*, 1501–1504, marble, height 17 ft. (517 cm), Accademia, Florence.

✦ PALAZZO VECCHIO
The Palazzo Vecchio was the Florentine seat of government. Begun in 1299, it went through a series of modifications between the thirteenth and sixteenth centuries. Today, the mayor of Florence and the city council still meet in the building.

✦ THE ROOM OF THE FIVE HUNDRED
This large room was added to the Palazzo Vecchio in 1494. It had to be large enough to hold the city's Grand Council, which had 500 members. Leonardo da Vinci and Michelangelo were hired to decorate the room by painting two victorious episodes in the history of the Florentine state. Neither of the works has survived.

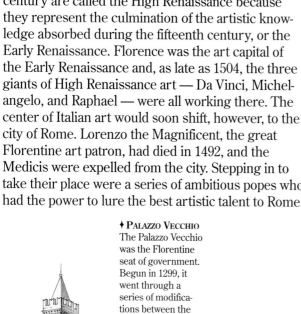

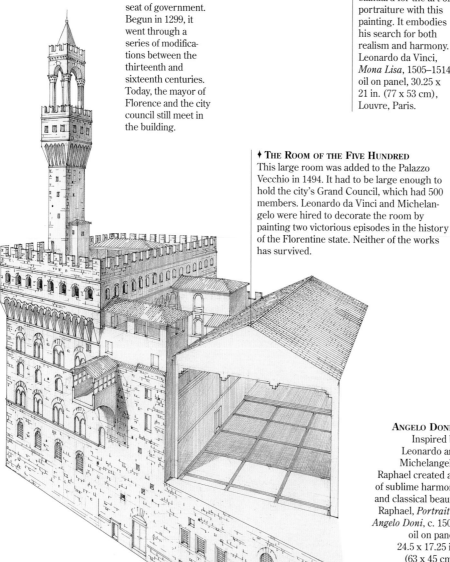

ANGELO DONI ✦
Inspired by Leonardo and Michelangelo, Raphael created art of sublime harmony and classical beauty. Raphael, *Portrait of Angelo Doni*, c. 1506, oil on panel, 24.5 x 17.25 in. (63 x 45 cm), Pitti Palace, Florence.

♦ DA VINCI

During the years he worked in Florence, Da Vinci recreated the art of portrait painting. His celebrated *Mona Lisa* (details left and right), with her softly lit face and hands, displays a naturalness and serenity that served as a model for generations of later artists.

♦ MICHELANGELO

Michelangelo had strong ties to Florence. He was raised there and was close to Lorenzo the Magnificent. In 1501, he was asked to create a statue that would symbolize Florentine strength and independence. He answered by transforming an enormous block of marble into *David* (details left and right).

♦ RAPHAEL

During his four years in Florence (1504–1508), Raphael executed a number of portraits for the families of the city's merchant aristocracy. Among them was a painting of the wealthy art patron Angelo Doni (details left and right). Inspired by Da Vinci, Raphael created a work where his subject dominates most of the painting, with a landscape visible in the distant background.

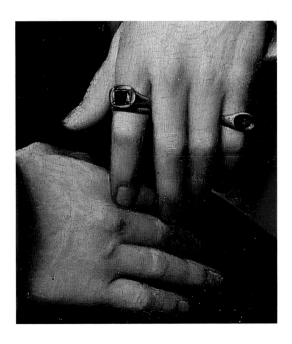

ROME

Julius II was elected pope in 1503. His papacy was notable for vigorous political and military campaigns to consolidate the Church's power, as well as a flourishing of the arts that made Rome the unrivaled center of High Renaissance culture. Julius commissioned projects from Bramante, including a new design for St. Peter's Basilica and the Belvedere Courtyard, where Julius assembled ancient relics uncovered during excavations in Rome. He summoned Raphael and Michelangelo to Rome to carry out important commissions at the Vatican. Julius II was succeeded by Leo X de Medici (1513–1521), who spent lavish sums making Rome a center of art and literature.

Above: Statue of the Emperor Claudius, first half of the first century A.D., marble, Vatican Museums, Rome.

✦ THE PAPACY IN THE EARLY SIXTEENTH CENTURY
The papacy played a pivotal role in Italian politics. In addition to being head of the Catholic Church, the pope was a secular ruler of territories in central Italy called the Papal States. The extent of the territories varied as other Italian city-states and foreign invaders vied to control them. Sometimes, the people of the territories rebelled against Rome. Julius II dealt decisively with all threats to his authority. His appetite for war earned him the nickname the "Warrior Pope." His successor, Leo X, was also embroiled in wars, battling threats from within Italy as well as from foreign aggressors.

Below: Raphael, *Portrait of Leo X* (detail), 1516–1519, tempera on panel, 60.5 x 47 in. (154 x 119 cm), Uffizi, Florence.

✦ SISTINE CHAPEL
Michelangelo painted the ceiling of the Sistine Chapel for Julius II between 1508 and 1512.

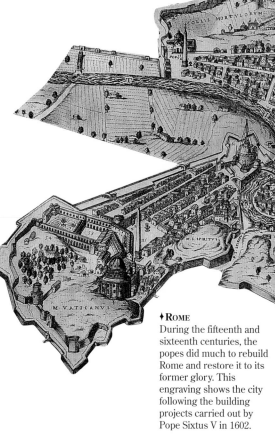

✦ ROME
During the fifteenth and sixteenth centuries, the popes did much to rebuild Rome and restore it to its former glory. This engraving shows the city following the building projects carried out by Pope Sixtus V in 1602.

THE NILE ✦
This Greek statue was unearthed in 1513 and purchased by Pope Leo X. It is now housed in the Vatican Museums in Rome.

SANTA MARIA ✦ SOPRA MINERVA
This church contains frescoes by Filippino Lippi, a statue by Michelangelo, and the tomb of painter Fra Angelico.

♦ GALATEA
Raphael depicted a scene from Greek mythology for the Roman villa of a wealthy Renaissance banker.
Raphael, *Galatea*, 1511, fresco, 9 ft. 8 in. x 7 ft. 5 in. (295 x 225 cm), Villa Farnesina, Rome.

♦ PALAZZO DELLA CANCELLERIA
Built between 1489 and 1513, this was the first Roman palazzo, or palace, built in the Renaissance style.

SAN PIETRO ♦ IN MONTORIO
This small temple known as the Tempietto is in the courtyard of the church of San Pietro in Montorio. It was designed by Bramante in 1503. Inspired by classical architecture and possessing harmonious proportions, it is a masterpiece of Renaissance architecture.

VENUS FELIX ♦
Pope Julius II purchased this statue in 1509, after it was unearthed in a square in Rome. The statue is now in the Vatican Museums in Rome.

♦ VILLA MEDICI
This Renaissance villa, built for a Medici cardinal, was one of the most elegant houses in Rome. It had a lavish garden and incorporated Roman statues excavated during the construction process.

PALAZZO FARNESE ♦
This impressive High Renaissance palace was begun in 1517 for Cardinal Alessandro Farnese, who later became pope. He hired Michelangelo to complete the palace's third story.

Above: Michelangelo, *Libyan Sibyl*, 1511, fresco, 12 ft. 11 in. x 12 ft. 6 in. (395 x 380 cm), Sistine Chapel, Vatican, Rome.

MICHELANGELO'S PROPHETS

Julius II invited Michelangelo to Rome in 1505 to design his tomb. While working on the tomb, Michelangelo received the commission to paint the Sistine Chapel ceiling. Both of these projects feature prophets — individuals who carry messages directly from God. For Julius II's tomb, Michelangelo chose the mighty figure of Moses, recognized by the Jewish and Christian traditions as the greatest prophet. In the Sistine Chapel, he painted seven Old Testament prophets and five sibyls, who were female prophets in antiquity. The figures in these works display both grandeur and spiritual intensity.

✦ MICHELANGELO IN ROME

Michelangelo was born near Arezzo in central Italy in 1475. As a young man, he lived and worked in the Florence of Lorenzo de Medici, but most of his later life was spent in Rome. He visited Rome for the first time in 1496, and in 1498 carved his celebrated *Pietà* there. In 1501, Pope Julius II summoned Michelangelo to Rome to create a monumental tomb for him, a work which would be ongoing for years. Between 1501–1504, he returned to Florence and produced *David*. Back in Rome, Michelangelo worked on the Sistine Chapel ceiling between 1508 and 1512. In 1547, at the height of his fame, he designed the dome of St. Peter's. He died in Rome in 1564.

Below: Michelangelo, *Delphic Sibyl*, 1511, fresco, 12 ft. 11 in. x 12 ft. 6 in. (395 x 380 cm), Sistine Chapel, Vatican, Rome.

✦ JONAH

This figure with a great fish beside him is the prophet Jonah. The Book of Jonah describes its hero as a reluctant prophet. When God summons him to go to Nineveh and denounce the people's sins, Jonah flees. Only after being swallowed by a great sea creature and spending three days in its belly does he decide to obey God. In Michelangelo's day, Christians interpreted Jonah's deliverance from the sea as a symbol of Christ's resurrection.

✦ MOSES

The original design for Pope Julius II's tomb called for forty statues on three levels, but the plan was reduced dramatically after the pope's death in 1513. In the final monument (above), the figure of Moses — the only statue that definitely can be attributed to Michelangelo — takes center stage. The figure's powerful form and noble gaze exemplify the Renaissance's glorification of humanity.

Michelangelo, *Moses*, 1515, marble, height 7 ft. 8.5 in. (235 cm), Church of San Pietro in Vincoli, Rome.

♦ **EZEKIEL**
Ezekiel was one of the four major Old Testament prophets. Here he sits in rapt attention, his body poised for action. Michelangelo used bright colors for his ceiling figures so they would be more visible to viewers standing on the floor.

JEREMIAH ♦
Jeremiah was charged with warning people of the coming wrath of God. Michelangelo depicted him as a figure full of sorrow and anguish.

♦ **ISAIAH**
Isaiah was the greatest Old Testament prophet, expressing his ideas through powerful imagery. Here, he appears to be listening intently.

DANIEL ♦
The last of the four major prophets of the Old Testament, Daniel is said to have survived the lion's den and other terrors. Here, he appears as a youthful figure, full of tense concentration.

♦ **ZECHARIAH**
Zechariah is called a minor prophet not because his messsage is less important than the major prophets, but because he wrote less. Here he appears to be reading from his book.

JOEL ♦
One of the earliest Old Testament prophets, Joel predicted an imminent Day of Judgment. Here, as he unfurls his scroll, he appears alarmed by the messsage it contains.

RAPHAEL AND THE VATICAN ROOMS

One of the major artistic projects commissioned by Pope Julius II was the decoration of four rooms, known as the Stanze, in the Vatican. Raphael was called to Rome in 1508 to replace the artists who had been working on the project. He completed the frescoes in the first two rooms, but the other rooms were finished by his assistants, notably Giulio Romano, after Raphael's premature death at the age of thirty-seven. The Stanze frescoes demonstrate Raphael's mastery of color and his talent for harmonious composition. Together with the Sistine Chapel frescoes, they rank among the masterpieces of High Renaissance art.

Above: Raphael, *Self-portrait*, 1506, oil on panel, 17 x 21 in. (43 x 53 cm), Uffizi, Florence.

✦ **RAPHAEL**
Raffaelo Sanzi, better known as Raphael, was born in Urbino in 1483. He was the son and pupil of the painter Giovanni Santi. At age twelve, he entered the work-shop of Perugino, Urbino's leading painter, where he studied the human figure. In Urbino, he also saw the work of Piero della Frances-ca and assimilated his mastery of space. At twenty-one, Raphael moved to Florence, where he met Da Vinci and Michelangelo. The influences of both artists can be seen in his work. In 1508, Bramante invited Raphael to Rome, where he received regular commissions from Julius II and Leo X. In 1517, he succeeded Bramante as chief architect of St. Peter's. Raphael died in Rome in 1520.

Below: Raphael, *Madonna of the Goldfinch*, 1507, oil on panel, 42 x 30 in. (107 x 77 cm), Uffizi, Florence.

✦ **HERACLITUS**
Detail from *The School of Athens* (left). The figure of Heraclitus, a Greek philosopher, is in fact Michelangelo, to whom Raphael is paying tribute.

✦ **PHILOSOPHY**
The theme of this painting, which faces the one on theology (below), is the triumph of intellect and rational truth. Raphael, *The School of Athens*, 1509–1510, fresco, base 27 feet (770 cm), Stanza della Segnatura, Vatican, Rome.

✦ **THEOLOGY**
The theme of this fresco is the triumph of theological truth. The painting spans both heaven and earth. In heaven, the figure of God is at the top. Jesus is in the middle, flanked by the Virgin Mary, St. John the Baptist, and other biblical figures. On earth, theologians, includ-ing Julius II, engage in debate. Raphael, *Disputation over the Sacrament,* 1509, fresco, base 27 feet (770 cm), Stanza della Segna-tura, Vatican, Rome.

♦ PLATO AND ARISTOTLE
Raphael placed the philosophers representing idealism and realism at the center of his composition. The face of Plato (left) is a portrait of Da Vinci. Detail from *The School of Athens.*

♦ DIOGENES
The position of Diogenes, sprawled across the steps, mirrors the ancient Greek philosopher's contempt for social values. Detail from *The School of Athens.*

♦ PYTHAGORAS
Pythagoras, the Greek philosopher and mathematician, is shown hard at work, with book, pen, and inkwell. Detail from *The School of Athens.*

♦THE POWER OF THE PAPACY
St. Peter was the first pope, and this scene of his liberation from prison alludes to the invincibility of the papacy. There is also an implicit glorification of Julius II.
Raphael, *The Liberation of St. Peter from Prison,* 1513–1514, fresco, base 21 ft. 8 in. (660 cm) Stanza di Eliodoro, Vatican, Rome.

Giovanni Bellini, *Portrait of Doge Loredan,* c. 1501, oil on panel, 24.5 x 17.75 in. (62 x 45 cm), National Gallery, London.

♦ THE CITY

Venice was founded in the sixth century when people on the mainland, fleeing from invaders, took refuge on a cluster of islands in a shallow lagoon at the head of the Adriatic Sea. Over time, they formed a league of villages and elected a leader, the Doge. Venice became a powerful city-state between the ninth and twelfth centuries. Because of its position on the Adriatic Sea, it developed a thriving trade with the East, particularly with the Byzantine Empire. By the end of the thirteenth century, Venice was the wealthiest and most powerful city in Europe. Its merchant families built lavish palaces along the Grand Canal. Over the centuries, Venice had become a formidable naval power in order to protect its trade routes. During the Renaissance, it was involved in wars with the Ottoman Turks, who captured Constantinople in 1453. It also battled other Italian city-states in an attempt to exert its influence on the mainland. Venice began losing power at the end of the Renaissance and fell into decline when Napoleon captured the city in 1797.

VENICE

The Renaissance was the Golden Age of Venetian art. Despite recurrent plagues and wars with the Ottoman Turks and other Italian city-states, the cultural life of the city thrived. Venetian painting reached its zenith during the High Renaissance, yet its style was quite different from that of Florence and Rome. Whereas the Florentine style was based on masterful drawing, Venetian art was distinguished by a virtuoso use of color. Although Venetian painters were excellent draftsmen, color and light were fundamental to their compositions. Artists in Venice had an advantage when it came to color. Because the city was a center of trade, they had access to a wide range of pigments coming from the East. Sometimes Venetian artists mixed crushed glass into their pigments to give their paintings a shimmering effect. Oil paints also became more common, providing luminous colors.

♦ THE OCCASION

Venice was a maritime republic whose power rested on its command of the seas. Each year, it acknowledged its special relationship to the sea with a "marriage" celebration. The event began with a regal procession of boats down the Grand Canal and out to the Adriatic Sea, where the Doge, or leader, of Venice threw a ring into the waters saying, "We marry you, O Sea, as a sign of our true and everlasting dominion."

THE BUCINTORO ♦

The procession was led by the Doge's ceremonial barge, called the Bucintoro. The Bucintoro was 98 feet (30 m) long and 26 feet (8 m) wide. It had two decks and was richly decorated.

♦ THE PROCESSION

With all of the bells in the city ringing, a throng of boats accompanies the Bucintoro on its procession from the Grand Canal toward the sea.

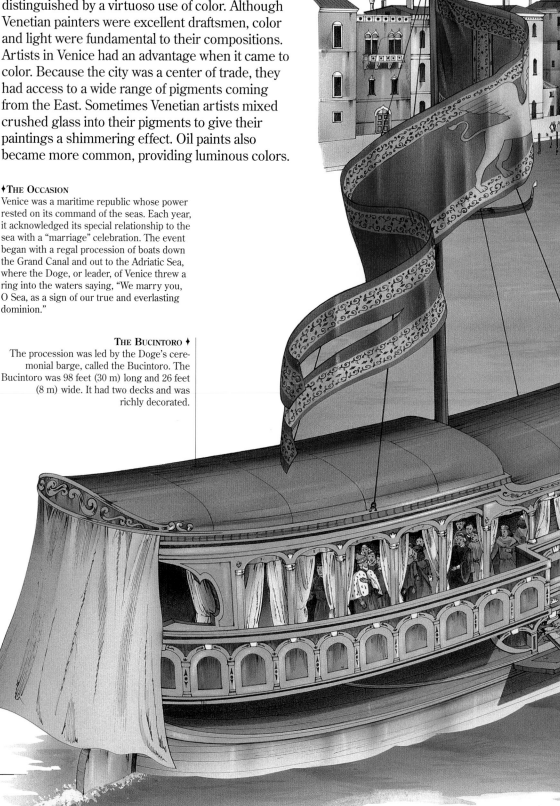

The Grand Canal is Venice's principal waterway. It follows a serpentine course through the heart of the city and ends at the Piazza San Marco, Venice's main square.

Above: Antonello da Messina, *Self-portrait*, 1473, oil on panel, 14 x 10 in. (35.5 x 25.5 cm, National Gallery, London.

✦VENETIAN ART
Renaissance Venice was one of the wonders of the world. Its unique-ness as an urban center rising from the water was matched by the distinctive character of its painting. Venetian art was shaped by a variety of outside influences. Because of its history of trade with the East, the Byzantine tradition played a significant role, and the influence of Islamic culture was also strong. During the fifteenth century, Venice had diplomatic and commercial relation-ships with the rest of Europe, particularly Flanders. Venice became a center for the import of Flem-ish paintings, which had a powerful effect on Italian artists.

Below: Antonello da Messina, *Annuncia-tion*, 1475, oil on panel, 18 x 13.5 in. (45 x 34.5 cm), Galleria Nazionale, Palermo.

✦JUSTICE
At the bow, or front, of the Bucintoro was a lion, the symbol of Venice, and a statue of Justice, holding the traditional symbol of a pair of scales.

✦ THE OARS
The Bucintoro was powered by oars. There were twenty-three oars on each side, each operated by three oarsmen on the lower deck. The oars moved in perfect unison.

GIOVANNI BELLINI

Giovanni Bellini was the great master of fifteenth-century Venetian painting. He came from a family of artists. Both his father and younger brother were painters, and his brother-in-law was Andrea Mantegna, the court painter of Mantua. In Bellini's youth, Venetian art was still dominated by the Gothic style of the fourteenth century, with its stylized, elongated figures. Inspired by other Italian artists, including Donatello, Piero della Francesca, and Antonello da Messina, Bellini changed the course of Venetian painting with his expressive, realistic figures, rich colors, and natural landscapes.

Giovanni Bellini, *Greek Madonna,* c. 1475, tempera on panel, 33 x 24.5 in. (84 x 62 cm), Brera, Milan.

♦ BELLINI'S LIFE AND ARTISTIC DEVELOPMENT

Giovanni Bellini was born around 1430. He was the son of the Venetian painter Jacopo Bellini and began his training in his father's studio. He was also influenced by the expressive sculpture of Donatello and the work of Andrea Mantegna, from whom he learned how to give the human figure structure and solidity. On his own, he developed a talent for color, a strong feeling for nature, and the ability to portray powerful human emotions. His landscapes are clearly based on the rural areas of the Venetian mainland. Between 1470 and 1473, while painting an altarpiece in Pesaro, Bellini visited the court of Urbino, where he was able to see the paintings of Piero della Francesca. These influenced his use of perspective. During the final years of his long life, he was appointed official painter to the Venetian Republic and continued to execute a large number of commissions. He died in 1516. Two of his pupils, Giorgione and Titian, would go on to become the leaders of sixteenth-century Venetian painting.

♦ POLYPTYCH

This polyptych (an altarpiece composed of several connected panels) hangs in the Church of Saints John and Paul in Venice.
Giovanni Bellini, *Polyptych of St. Vincent Ferrer.* Before 1464.
Top: Angel of the Annunciation, Dead Christ Supported by Angels, Virgin Mary; panels, each 28.5 x 26.5 in. (72 x 67 cm); Middle: St. Christopher, St. Vincent Ferrer, St. Sebastian; panels, each 14.25 x 23.5 in. (36 x 60 cm). Bottom: five episodes from the life of Vincent Ferrer; panels, each 14.25 x 23.5 in. (36 x 60 cm).

♦ THE DEAD CHRIST

Bellini infused his religious paintings with tremendous depth of feeling.
Giovanni Bellini, *Dead Christ Supported by Mary and St. John the Evangelist (Pietà),* 1467 (whole above, detail left), Brera, Milan.

AN EARLIER WORK ♦

Dead Christ Supported by Two Angels (Pietà), c. 1452, panel, 29 x 19.75 in. (74 x 50 cm), Correr Museum, Venice.

ST. MARK'S SQUARE ✦
This work, by Bellini's brother, features the grand urban space of St. Mark's Square, a frequent subject of Venetian paintings. Gentile Bellini, *Procession in St. Mark's Square*, 1496, Accademia, Venice.

LANDSCAPE ✦
In this work, Bellini introduced an innovative horizontal format with a panoramic landscape. *Madonna and Child*, 1508, Brera, Milan.

Above and below: Giovanni Bellini, San Giobbe altarpiece, c. 1478–1480, panel, 15 ft. 5 in. x 8 ft. 5 in. (471 x 258 cm), Accademia, Venice.

✦THE INFLUENCE OF ANTONELLO DA MESSINA
Antonello da Messina (1430–1479) worked in Naples, where he probably first came into contact with Flemish painting. During the Renaissance, Italian city-states engaged in active trade with Flanders, and Italian merchants often brought back samples of Flemish art. Antonello was a master of detail in the Flemish manner and a gifted and prolific portrait painter. In 1475, he arrived in Venice, where Giovanni Bellini and others learned from his command of oil painting techniques. At the time, oil paints were new and Antonello is credited with introducing them to Venice. Bellini's San Giobbe altarpiece shows his artistic debt to Antonello.

A MASTER OF ✦ PORTRAITURE
The three-quarter view was a characteristic of Flemish portrait painting. Antonello da Messina, *Condottiere*, 1475, oil on panel, 13.75 x 11 inches (35 x 28 cm), Louvre, Paris.

✦PORTRAIT BY BELLINI
Giovanni Bellini, *Portrait of a Man*, 1480–1490, panel, 13 x 10 inches (32.8 x 25.5 cm), Louvre, Paris.

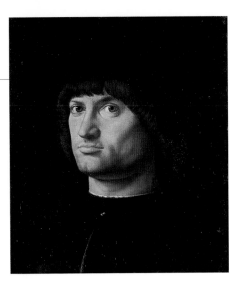

GIORGIONE

Giorgione and Titian, the two great innovators of sixteenth-century Venetian art, both spent time in Giovanni Bellini's workshop. Giorgione went even further than Bellini in the creation of realistic landscapes. The prominence of landscapes in his work and his rich depiction of nature were innovative for the time. His work also displays a freedom of composition. Instead of the clear outlines common in central Italian painting, Giorgione used shades of color to differentiate between objects. This gives his work a soft, subtle beauty and atmospheric quality.

Giorgione, *Enthroned Madonna and Child*, 1504–1505, panel, 78.75 x 60 in. (200 x 152 cm), San Liberale, Castelfranco Veneto.

✦ GIORGIONE

Giorgione was born in Castelfranco Veneto, near Venice, in about 1478. He served in the workshop of Giovanni Bellini. Around 1504, he painted an innovative altarpiece (above) for the church of San Liberale in Castelfranco. The firgures were not enclosed in an architectural framework, as they always had been in the past, but were arranged in the shape of a pyramid with a wide landscape in the background. In 1508, Giorgione painted *The Three Philosophers*. The composition is asymmetrical with a vast landscape occupying the left half of the painting. Landscapes figure prominently in Giorgione's work, even if they have little to do with the subject. Giorgione died of the plague in Venice in 1510. He signed few paintings, so many of his works remain unknown. Below: detail from *The Three Philosophers*, 1508, oil on canvas, 48.5 x 57 in. (123.5 x 144.5 cm), Kunsthistorisches Museum, Vienna.

✦ NATURE

Nature dominates this small canvas, with the storm playing a prominent role. While the meaning of the figures is unclear, Giorgione has integrated them into the background. Trees, clouds, the bridge, and the human figures are all parts of a unified whole. *The Tempest*, 1506–1508, oil on canvas, 30 x 29 in. (82 x 73 cm), Accademia, Venice.

✦ THE TEMPEST

Like many of Giorgione's works, the meaning of *The Tempest* is obscure and has been the object of considerable debate among art scholars. Some interpret the scene as entirely a product of the artist's imagination. Others believe the painting is full of symbolism. Some find its source in stories from antiquity. At the time Giorgione was working, the printing industry was thriving in Venice and publications of classical texts were readily available. Regardless of the painting's meaning, *The Tempest* is notable for its striking landscape. Far from being a mere backdrop, nature is an integral part of the composition. Giorgione's rich colors and stormy sky lend drama to the scene. Landscapes were not a dominant feature of central Italian art, but they took on new prominence in the hands of Venetian painters.

Titian, *Self-portrait*,
1565–1570, detail, oil
on canvas, 34 x 25.5
in. (86 x 65 cm),
Prado, Madrid.

TITIAN

Following the deaths of Bellini and Giorgione, Titian
became the undisputed master of Venetian painting.
His work dominated Venetian art during the sixteenth
century, which was the peak of the Renaissance in
Venice. Titian was an extremely versatile painter.
He excelled at portraiture as well as landscapes. He
brought new vigor to religious art and created
dynamic portrayals of allegories and myths. He was
a master colorist whose fame spread throughout
Europe. His clients included the ruling houses of
Italy, the Holy Roman Emperor, and the king of Spain.

✦ THE MYTH
Titian, *Danae,*
1553–1554, oil on
canvas, 50.25 x 70 in.
(128 x 178 cm),
Prado, Madrid.

✦ THE EMPEROR
Titian, *Charles V on
Horseback*, 1548, oil
on canvas, 10 ft. 10
in. x 9 ft. (332 x 279
cm), Prado, Madrid.

✦ TITIAN
Titian's life and
career span nearly
the entire sixteenth
century. He was
born in Pieve di
Cadore, a town in the
Veneto, around 1490
and died in Venice in
1576. After working
as an apprentice to
Gentile and Giovanni
Bellini, he came into
contact with
Giorgione, in whose
paintings color plays
a dominant role.
Titian's own style
became distin-
guished by its
dramatic color, in
particular, its brilliant
reds, and the
naturalness of his
human figures. After
the deaths of
Giorgione in 1510
and Giovanni Bellini
in 1516, Titian
became the leading
figure in Venetian
painting. In addition
to private commis-
sions, he received
many public projects.
He was celebrated
not only in Venice,
but throughout Italy
and in the ruling
houses of Europe. In
1545, after working
for the lords of
Ferrara and Urbino,
he was triumphantly
received in Rome by
Pope Paul III. From
1550, he worked for
Charles V, the Holy
Roman Emperor, and
his son Philip II, the
king of Spain. Titian
remained active and
received commis-
sions until the end of
his life. He died in
Venice while a plague
was raging in the city.
His work inspired
many later artists.

✦ THE POPE
Titian, *Pope Paul III with Alessandro and
Ottavio Farnese,* 1546, oil on canvas, 6 ft. 10
in. x 5 ft. 8 in. (210 x 174 cm), Capodimonte
Gallery, Naples.

✦ THE ASSUMPTION
With his monumental *Assumption*, Titian
revolutionized altar painting, injecting it with new
emotional energy. His composition gives Mary's
assumption a sense of soaring movement,
reinforced by the gestures of the crowd below.
His masterful use of color plays a key role in
binding the various parts into a unified whole.
The painting took two years to complete and it
established Titian's reputation.
Titian, *Assumption of the Virgin*, 1516–1518, oil on
panel, 22 ft. 6 in. x 11 ft. 10 in. (690 x 360 cm),
Church of Santa Maria Gloriosa dei Frari, Venice.

THE LOW COUNTRIES

Rabbit Hunting with a Ferret, c. 1560, detail, 9 ft. 10 in. x 11 ft. 10 in. (300 x 360 cm), M. H. De Young Museum, San Francisco.

Early in the fifteenth century, at about the same time the Renaissance was beginning in Florence, Flanders experienced a similar flourishing of the arts. Flanders was the wealthiest province in the Low Countries and its cities, including Bruges, Ghent, and Brussels, were thriving centers of commerce. Italian banks and businesses had branches in Flanders and Italian merchants brought Flemish art back to Italy. Both Italian and Flemish artists benefited from the cultural exchange. Like Florence, the merchant classes played a dominant role in the region's political, economic, and cultural life. They commissioned paintings and tapestries to decorate their homes and public buildings. Flanders' prosperity was built on the textile trade and it was the center of European tapestry-making.

✦ A TURBULENT ERA
The Low Countries had a turbulent political history, with various European powers vying for their control. For much of the fifteenth century, they were ruled by the Duchy of Burgundy. At the time, Burgundy was not part of France, and its wealth and brilliant court life rivaled that of the French kingdom. The Burgundian nobles lived mainly in the trading centers of Bruges, Ghent, and Brussels. They were active patrons of the arts and kept many Flemish painters and tapestry makers busy with commissions. The last Burgundian ruler, Mary, married Maximilian I of Austria, a Habsburg. When she died in 1489, the Low Countries passed to the Habsburgs. They were later inherited by Maximilian's grandson, Charles V, the Holy Roman Emperor. He ruled during the first half of the sixteenth century. In 1556, his son, Phillip II, King of Spain, inherited the Low Countries. Spain subjected them to heavy taxes and religious persecution and the Low Countries rebelled, beginning a long war with Spain.

| Friesland |
| Groningen |
| Overijssel |
| Utrecht |
| Holland | Gelderland |
| Zeeland | Spanish Gelderland |
| Land of the Generality |
| Flanders |
Brabant	Maastricht
Namur	Limburg
Artois	Hainaut
Luxembourg

✦ THE LOW COUNTRIES
The Low Countries were in an area of low-lying land in northwestern Europe. They consisted of seventeen provinces and covered an area corresponding roughly to present-day Belgium, the Netherlands, and Luxembourg. Flanders was the wealthiest province and its name is often used to denote the entire region.

✦ TAPESTRIES
Tapestries are large, hand-woven wall hangings. They were used to decorate the walls of palaces and large public buildings. Kings and nobles spent huge sums of money on tapestries, and some of the most talented Renaissance artists created designs for them. The Low Countries were an important center of tapestry-making from the fifteenth to the seventeenth century.

HORIZONTAL LOOM ✦
The lengthwise yarns, called the warp, are stretched on the loom. The heddles, which lift the threads, are operated by pedals. The design is placed under the warp so the loomworkers can follow it as they weave.

♦ TAPESTRY WEAVING
Tapestry weaving is regarded as an art form. It requires skill and sensitivity in the choice of colors and materials. Wool, silk, and linen were used, as well as gold and silver threads. The designs were often created by famous painters.

♦ DYEING
The yarns are immersed in vats containing alum, which acts as a fixing agent, and dye powders: saffron for the yellows, indigo for the blues, and Brazilian wood for the deep reds.

THE COMMISSION ♦
While his friends admire a nearby tapestry, the client agrees on a price and delivery date with the workshop master.

♦ APPRENTICES
Before being promoted to work on the loom, apprentices had to learn all the stages involved in making a tapestry. Apprenticeships were long and regulated by strict rules.

VERTICAL LOOM ♦
The threads of the warp are stretched between two large rollers operated by levers. The tapestry weaver works on the back of the tapestry, using a mirror in front to check his progress.

FIFTEENTH-CENTURY FLEMISH PAINTING

Above: Hubert and Jan van Eyck, *Adoration of the Lamb,* detail.

Flemish painting is notable for its extreme realism and its depiction of light. Italian painters focused on perspective and classical proportion to portray their subjects. Flemish painters depicted subjects by paying meticulous attention to detail. Both their interiors and landscapes are full of details, with objects in the background being as carefully rendered as those in the foreground. Some Flemish paintings contained symbolism, in which an orindary object carried a double meaning. Painters such as Jan van Eyck were masters at creating realistic interiors. In his work, light entering from a window appears as real as the light reflected on a chandelier or the surface of a mirror.

♦ **THE INFLUENCE OF FLEMISH PAINTERS**
Art historians have identified three fundamental qualities in Flemish painting of the fifteenth century: a meticulous realism, a brilliant rendering of light, and multiple symbolic meanings, concealed in everyday objects. The influence of Flemish painting in Italy, particularly in the south, was related not to its symbolism, but to its realism and treatment of light. The impact of Flemish painting was also felt outside Italy: in Provence, in the Rhine Valley, and in Spain. The Italian artist who most assimilated the realism of the Flemish masters was Antonello da Messina. Flemish influence was also apparent in the landscapes of Piero della Francesca and Giovanni Bellini. Italian merchants who had lived in Flanders helped to spread knowledge of Flemish painting throughout Italy. So, too, did Italian ruling families, who brought celebrated Flemish artists to their courts. Italian art also made its way into Flanders. Artists learned new techniques from each other, but the overall styles of each region remained distinct.

♦ **ROBERT CAMPIN**
Campin (1378–1444) was the first Flemish painter to render objects in minute detail. The use of a window with a landscape in the distance adds depth to the interior and became a characteristic of Flemish painting. *Virgin and Child Before a Firescreen,* 1420–1425, tempera on panel, 25 x 19 in. (63 x 48 cm), National Gallery, London.

♦ **THE VAN EYCKS**
This work, also known as the *Ghent Altarpiece,* is considered Hubert van Eyck's masterpiece. Begun in about 1420, he worked on it until his death in 1426. It was finished by his younger brother Jan in 1432. The altarpiece was commissioned by a wealthy Flemish merchant. It consists of twelve panels. Eight of the outer, hinged panels are painted on the back. The complex composition is unified by the light of an enchanted landscape.
Hubert van Eyck (c. 1366–1426), *Adoration of the Lamb,* 1420–1432, whole above and detail left, oil on panel, 54. 2 x 95.4 in. (137.7 x 242.3 cm), Cathedral of St. Bavon, Ghent.

♦AN ITALIAN MERCHANT
One of the most famous paintings in Western art, this portrait of an Italian merchant living in Bruges is intensely realistic and full of symbols. Though their meaning has been debated, the clothing, furnishings, and even the oranges point to a life of wealth and luxury. Jan van Eyck, *Giovanni Arnolfini and His Wife,* 1434, oil on panel, 32.25 x 23.6 in. (82 x 60 cm), National Gallery. London.

Above: Jan van Eyck, *Portrait of Margaret van Eyck* (the artist's wife), 1439, detail, oil on panel, 16.2 x 13.6 in. (41.2 x 34.6 cm), Groeninge-museum, Bruges.

♦JAN VAN EYCK
Jan van Eyck was considered the greatest Flemish painter of his day. He was a master of the Flemish style, depicting people, objects, and land-scapes with great realism and extreme attention to detail. He was also able to reproduce the effects of light on all types of surfaces. Beginning in 1425, he worked in Bruges in the service of Philip III, a powerful duke of Burgundy. In addition to his artistic activity, the duke sent Van Eyck on diplomatic missions. Van Eyck achieved both fame and wealth during his lifetime. He died in Bruges in 1441.

ROGIER ♦ VAN DER WEYDEN
Rogier van der Weyden was born near Brussels around 1400. A pupil of Robert Campin, his paintings were very expressive and often highly dramatic. He was well-connected to the Burgundian families in Brussels, whose patronage brought him both wealth and fame throughout Europe. *Descent from the Cross,* c. 1435, oil on panel, 86.6 x 103 in. (220 x 262 cm), Prado, Madrid.

♦ LATE FIFTEENTH-CENTURY PAINTERS
These two artists exemplify the great variety of Flemish art. Left: Hieronymus Bosch (c.1453–516), *Prodigal Son,* c. 1510, oil on canvas, diameter 27.8 in. (70.6 cm), Boymansvan Beuningen Museum, Rotterdam.
Right: Hans Memling (1435–1494), *Reliquary of St. Ursula,* 1489, detail, oil on panel, Hans Memling Museum, Bruges.

Above: Robert Campin, *St. Veronica*, c. 1430, detail, oil on panel, Stadelsches Kunstinsitut, Frankfurt.

Campin is known as the first master of Flemish painting. His work is full of the realistic details that became the hall-mark of the style.

OIL PAINTING

Above: Presumed self-portrait of Jan van Eyck, *Man in a Turban*, 1433, oil on panel, 10 x 7.5 in. (25.5 x 19 cm), National Gallery, London.

Painting with oils originated in northern Europe, perhaps as early as the twelfth century. It wasn't until the fifteenth century, however, that oils were widely used. It was Jan van Eyck and other Flemish painters who popularized the technique and demonstrated its capabilties. Oil paints are trans-lucent, allowing painters to achieve more luminous colors. They can also be applied very thinly, which enabled Flemish painters to capture the subtle effects of light. Italian painters were still using tempera, but once they saw what Flemish artists had achieved, they began switching to oil paints. By the sixteenth century, oils had replaced tem-pera as the preferred medium of European artists.

♦ FROM TEMPERA TO OIL

Until the fifteenth century, tempera was almost the only medium used in European painting. Tempera consists of ground pigments mixed with egg yolk and water. The egg causes tempera to dry quickly, making it difficult to blend colors and restrict-ing artists in the types of brush-strokes they could use. With oil painting, pigments are blended with slow-drying oils, such as linseed or walnut oil. They are much more versatile than tempera. Their slower drying time allowed artists to blend colors and use a variety of brush-strokes to achieve different textures. Because oils can be applied thinly, artists could build up layers of paint to get richer colors. Layers of translucent oils were also used as glazes, to give the surface of paintings a glossy look. Tempera, by contrast, resulted in flatter colors and a matte surface. Oil painting spread to Italy in the second half of the fifteenth century. Italian artists who pioneered the new technique were Antonello da Messina, Leonardo da Vinci, and the Venetian painters.

CARPENTRY ♦
The panels are held together with dovetail joints and reinforced at the back with a wooden frame.

VISITORS ♦
Two wealthy art patrons arrive at Van Eyck's workshop, where his many pupils and assistants are at work.

MANNEQUINS ♦
To provide models for the length of time needed to complete the work, mannequins with plastic garments are used.

A WORK IN ♦ PROGRESS
An assistant applies color glazes to Van Eyck's painting of *The Madonna of Chancellor Rolin,* while two young pupils draw from the models. A workshop assistant prepares the colors.

♦ **JAN VAN EYCK**
The Madonna of Chancellor Rolin, 1433–1434,
oil on panel, 26 x 23.6 in. (66 x 62 cm), Louvre,
Paris. Nicolas Rolin, left, chancellor to Philip
III of Burgundy, commissioned the work.

♦ **THE WINDOW**
The positions of the
figures direct our gaze
to the landscape
beyond the arches of
the loggia, or open-air,
rooftop room.

♦ **LIGHTING**
A subtle play of light
from many sources:
the arches, the side
windows, and even
the gold brocade of
Rolin's garment.

THE MASTER ♦
The painter Jan van
Eyck, sitting with his
back to us, studies
the features of a
well-to-do lady
whose portrait he is
about to paint.

WOOD SAMPLES ♦
Artists painted on
panels made of oak,
lime, beech, poplar,
birch, or cedar. The
wood might come
from barrels or
the planks of
old ships.

BRUEGEL

Pieter Bruegel the Elder is famous for his masterful paintings of peasants. He was active during the middle of the sixteenth century — a time when painting scenes of everyday village life was extremely rare. Bruegel's paintings are full of realistic detail, from villagers' gestures and facial expressions to the clothes they wore and the food they ate. He used dark, earthy colors appropriate to his subject matter. One of his most famous paintings depicts a variety of children's games, yet the mood of the painting is not sentimental. It is an accurate representation of life as Bruegel saw it. Bruegel's realism is in keeping with the painting tradition of the Low Countries, yet he developed a style that was uniquely his own.

Pieter Bruegel, *Self-portrait*, c.1565, detail, drawing in pen and ink, 9.8 x 8.5 in. (25 x 21.6 cm), Albertina, Vienna.

♦ PIETER BRUEGEL THE ELDER

Pieter Bruegel was probably born in Breda, in what is now the southern Netherlands, around 1525. He traveled to Italy and France, but he was largely influenced by the work of other Flemish artists. Bruegel's paintings display the realism and attention to detail that were hallmarks of the Flemish style. He studied and worked in Antwerp and later settled in Brussels. Antwerp was a vibrant center of publishing and Bruegel's early work there consisted of drawings and engravings. He eventually concentrated on painting. The most common themes for his paintings were landscapes and crowds of people. Three of his most famous works are *Flemish Proverbs* (1559), *Battle Between Carnival and Lent* (1559), and *Children's Games* (1560). All contain narratives and all are overflowing with people and activity. Bruegel is known as "the Elder" because he had two sons who also became painters: Pieter the Younger, born in 1564, and Jan, born in 1568. Pieter Bruegel the Elder died in Brussels in 1569.

♦ PERSPECTIVE

The red perspective lines above show that the chaos of the scene is under artistic control. The lines act as a basis for the structure of the composition.

♦ NARRATIVE PAINTING

In this painting, Bruegel crowded a great many people and activities into a single scene. His ability to depict everyday life in all its details was remarkable. Looking at this work, it is possible to learn a great deal about village life in the Low Countires during the sixteenth century. The painting includes over eighty different children's games, some of which are still popular today.

Pieter Bruegel the Elder, *Children's Games,* 1560, whole above, detail right, oil on panel, 46.5 x 63.4 in. (118 x 161 cm), Kunsthistorisches Museum, Vienna.

♦ EIGHTY-FOUR GAMES
These six scenes are details from Bruegel's painting *Children's Games.* The painting illustrates eighty-four children's games that were popular during the sixteenth century. Shown here are, clockwise from top left: running with a hoop; riding piggyback; swinging on a rail; whipping a top; guessing which hand; spinning in circles and climbing trees.

GLUTTONY ♦
Three men — a peasant, a soldier, and a priest — have been lured by the delights of gluttony. They lie under the Tree of Plenty while a fourth man sits under a roof of pies and various edibles wander about. Pieter Bruegel the Elder, *The Land of Cockaigne*, 1567, oil on panel, 20.5 x 28.3 in. (52 x 72 cm), Alte Pinakothek, Munich.

♦ AN ORDERLY CROWD
Like *Children's Games*, this work is filled with people and activity, yet it doesn't feel cluttered or confusing. This is due to Bruegel's careful arrangement of the scene. By placing the table at an angle, he has organized the figures into clear spaces, such as the foreground and the background. It is thought that Bruegel painted his own portrait in the figure of the well-dressed man conversing with a monk at the end of the table.
Pieter Bruegel the Elder, *Peasant Wedding*, c. 1568, whole above and detail, above left, oil on panel, 45 x 64 in. (114 x 163 cm), Kunsthistorisches Museum, Vienna.

GERMANY

Renaissance ideas were brought to Germany by German artists who had traveled to Italy. While Germany produced some well-known painters, its greatest contribution to the spread of humanism was the development of moveable type in the mid-fifteenth century. Prior to that time, books were written by hand or printed by the woodblock method, in which the text and illustrations for an entire page were carved into a single wooden block. With moveable type, each letter was a separate piece that could be arranged with other letters to form words. Johann Gutenberg invented the first moveable type in Europe and used it to produce his famous Bible in Mainz in 1455. His method of producing pages was both quick and economical and led to similar efficiencies in printing. All of these developments contributed to the spread of art and ideas throughout Europe.

Albrecht Dürer, *The Emperor Maximilian I,* 1519, oil on panel, 29 x 24.2 in. (74 x 61.5 cm), Kunsthistorisches Museum, Vienna.

✦ GERMANY
During the fourteenth and fifteenth centuries, Germany was a patchwork of independent states ruled by princes. The states were part of the Holy Roman Empire, which was founded by the German king Otto I in 962 and included the territories of present-day Germany and Austria and other northern European countries. It was ruled by an emperor, who viewed the empire as a continuation of the original Roman Empire in the West. The emperors themselves, however, had little authority and clashes between the emperor and the princes were common. As German cities became more prosperous, they, too, began to exercise more power in political affairs. The coronation of Charles V as Holy Roman Emperor in 1519 coincided with the Protestant Reformation. The Reformation began in Germany as a religious protest against papal abuses and certain doctrines and practices within the Catholic Church. It had repercussions throughout Europe. In the Holy Roman Empire, it pitted German Protestant princes against the Roman Catholic emperor, and would lead greatly to the shrinking and weakening of the empire itself.

✦ THE SCHONGAUER WORKSHOP
Martin Schongauer (1450–1491) was a German painter and engraver. His paintings showed the influence of Flemish art and were much admired during his lifetime, but he is best-known today for his engravings. Schongauer was the son of a goldsmith, from whom he learned engraving techniques. His workshop perfected the art of engraving and printed large, high-quality editions of his work, which circulated throughout Europe.

THE FORM ✦
A metal form holds two pages to be printed.

THE ARTIST ✦
German artist Albrecht Dürer copies his original drawing onto a block of wood. The wood will be used to make the engraving.

THE ENGRAVING ✦
A craftsman uses a small knife to carve the design into the block. Another worker uses a hammer and chisel to cut away parts of the block that won't be used.

INKS ✦
Young apprentices prepare the inks. The apprentices are often the sons or grandsons of older workers who wish to pass on their craft to a family member. Even the sons of the workshop master must start with the humblest of jobs.

♦ **COLMAR**
The Schongauer workshop looked onto a street in the German town of Colmar.

♦ **TYPESETTING**
A typesetter makes up a page while seated at the box where the moveable blocks of type are kept. A colleague in front of him measures the line of text he has composed.

♦ **THE PRINTING PRESS**
Cotton wads are used to spread ink onto the printing blocks. A clean sheet of paper is arranged on the form before being passed through the press.

♦ **MAP OF GERMANY**
Many German cities were important artistic centers during the Renaissance.

PAPER ♦
Some printed proofs lie next to a stack of blank paper. One of the Schongauer brothers checks a printed sample.

WOOD SCULPTURE

German wood sculpture of the late fifteenth century was a major European art. Its leading practitioners are less famous today than the painters of their time, yet they took the art of wood carving to new heights, particularly in their creation of magnificent winged altarpieces. Altarpieces were used to decorate the space behind a church altar. The wings were hinged panels that could be opened on special occasions. These ornately carved works combined sculpture, painting, and architecture and were often enormous. The one created by Veit Stoss for St. Mary's Church in Krakow, Poland (pictured below), reached a height of almost fifty feet (15 meters).

✦THE FIRST CUT
A carpenter uses a hatchet to rough out the form of a statue from a piece of wood. The wood was usually a halved section of a tree trunk. Other tools, such as axes, mallets, and chisels, will be used to create the contours of the figure.

✦THE SHELL
The wooden figure is hollowed out inside so the wood won't crack as it ages. Lime paste and plaster are used to fill small cracks or to make repairs.

✦POLISHING
When the surface is dry, the statue is polished to make it smooth. It is then ready to be painted.

✦THE SURFACE
Many thin layers of plaster, glue, and hardening agents are applied to the surface of the statue. Some areas are covered with fabric.

✦THE SUMMIT
The altarpiece is crowned with small figures and a wealth of delicate carvings that add height and lightness to the work.

✦THE FIGURES
The free-standing figures would be colorfully painted.

THE WINGS ✦
The two hinged wings were decorated with painted bas-reliefs. The wings were opened only on feast days or for special ceremonies.

THE CORPUS ✦
The corpus was the central focus of the altarpiece. It was heavily carved and could be covered by closing the wings.

THE PREDELLA ✦
The predella was the base of the altarpiece. Its purpose was to raise the sculpture to a height where it would be visible from a distance. The predella was carved and decorated.

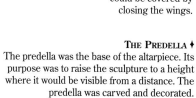

Above and below:
Michel Erhart, *St.
John the Evangelist*,
c. 1493, details,
Monastery Church,
Blaubeuren.

✦ VEIT STOSS

Considered one of the greatest wood carvers of the sixteenth century, Veit Stoss was born in or near Nuremberg, Germany, around 1447. Between 1477 and 1496, he lived in Krakow, Poland, where he ran a successful workshop producing pieces for the Polish court. It was during this period that he made the magnificent high altar for St. Mary's Church (left) in Krakow. He also carved many tombs, including one for King Casimir IV of Poland in 1492. He later returned to Nuremberg and continued working in southern Germany until his death in 1533.

✦THE BAMBERG ALTAR

High altar, 1520–1523,
wood sculpture,
carpentry in firwood,
carving in limewood,
height 11 ft. 8 in.
(355 cm), Cathedral,
Bamberg, Germany.

✦ CITIES OF THE WOOD CARVERS

Central Europe, and southern Germany in particular, were centers of wood sculpture during the Renaissance. Some of the most important cities were Strasbourg, Freiburg, Basel, Ulm, Nuremburg, Munich, Krakow, and Prague. In Germany, carved altarpieces had been popular since the late Middle Ages and they reached new heights during the Renaissance. Italian altarpieces, by contrast, were usually large paintings. German altarpieces were monumental flights of fancy, adorned with florid carvings from top to bottom. Yet the work done by woodcarvers was not always on such a grand scale. Much of it consisted of small items, such as candelabras, figurines, and objects used for private devotion. Even the smallest sculptures, however, were filled with expert carving and rich detail.

GERMAN PAINTERS

The height of German Renaissance painting occurred during the first three decades of the sixteenth century. Although German artists were exposed to Italian art, German painting had its own distinct identity, marked by an intense emotional expressiveness. Religion was a common theme of German art, both before and during the Reformation. German painters also excelled at portrait painting. Germany was a center of printing and many painters were also skilled engravers. The most famous German artist of the Renaissance was Albrecht Dürer. His painting style was influenced by trips to Italy, but it was his engraving that brought him fame throughout Europe.

Above: *Albrecht of Brandenburg Before the Crucifix,* 1520–1525, panel, Alte Pinakothek, Munich.

♦ **LUCAS CRANACH**
Cranach was born in Kronach, in southern Germany, in 1472. He was known for his woodcuts as well as his paintings. Much of his work dealt with religious subject matter, though he was equally adept at portrait painting. He painted a famous portrait of Martin Luther, the leader of the Protestant Reformation. He died in 1553.

Above: *Crucifixion,* c. 1520, panel, Museum of Art, Budapest.

♦ **ALBRECHT ALTDORFER**
Altdorfer was born around 1480 in Regensberg, a town in southern Germany located on the Danube River. Altdorfer was a pioneer of landscape painting and became the leader of a group of painters known as the Danube school. He was also known for his expressive religious paintings. He produced engravings and woodcuts as well as paintings. He died in Germany in 1538.

♦ **ADAM AND EVE**
Dürer painted these two panels shortly after returning to Nuremberg from his second visit to Italy. While in Italy, he devoted himself to the study of perspective, anatomy, and proportion. These were the first life-size nudes in German painting. For Dürer, they represented the ideal proportions of the human body.
Albrecht Dürer, *Adam and Eve*, 1507, oil on panel; each 82 x 32 in. (209 x 81 cm), Prado, Madrid.

♦ **DÜRER'S LAST WORKS**
These two panels were painted in the final years of Dürer's life, when he worked on a series of paintings with religious themes. *Four Apostles*, 1526, oil on panel, 85 x 30 in. (215.5 x 76 cm), Alte Pinakothek, Munich.

♦ **PLAY OF ARCHES**
In this work by Dürer, the figures are arranged almost as if they were on a stage. Perspective plays a major role in the painting and is underscored by the placement of the arches. The subtle interplay of the arches is the most striking feature of the work.
Albrecht Dürer, *Adoration of the Magi*, 1504, whole above, detail left, 39.4 x 45 in. (100 x 114 cm), Uffizi, Florence.

Above: Albrecht Dürer, *Self-portrait,* 1500, panel, Alte Pinakothek, Munich.

♦ **ALBRECHT DÜRER**
Dürer was born in Nuremberg in 1471 and died there in 1528. He was a painter, engraver, and mathematician. His engravings made him famous throughout Europe. He took two trips to Italy, where he met Bellini and other Italian masters who influenced his painting style. He also published books on math and human proportion.

♦ **MATHIAS GRÜNEWALD**
Grünewald was born between 1470 and 1480 and died in 1528. Most of his known works are religious in theme and consist of multiple panels. His most celebrated work is the Isenheim altarpiece, which contains twelve panels. The work is marked by bold colors and distorted figures whose faces express intense emotion. The figure of Jesus is particularly striking, showing tortured hands opened in a spasm of pain.
Crucifixion with Saints Anthony and Sebastian (from the Isenheim altarpiece), 1512–1516, oil on panel, Unterlinden Museum, Colmar.

♦ **TRIPTYCH**
In this triptych, the Nativity is flanked by St. George, left, and St. Eustace, right.
Albrecht Dürer, *Nativity*, 1504, oil on panel, Alte Pinakothek, Munich.

Above: Hans Holbein, *Portrait of Erasmus of Rotterdam*, 1523, tempera on panel, Louvre, Paris.

♦ **HANS HOLBEIN THE YOUNGER**
Holbein was the last great figure of the German Renaissance. He was born in Augsburg, in southern Germany, in 1497. For a time, he worked in Basel, Switzerland, painting altarpieces. He left Basel in 1532 for England. There, his talent for portraits was quickly recognized and he became official court portrait painter to King Henry VIII. He was named court fashion designer as well. Holbein died in London in 1543.

FRANCE

The Renaissance reached France at the end of the fifteenth century. The French king Charles VIII invaded the Italian peninsula in 1494, and when he returned to France, he brought Italian artists with him. Their influence can be seen in the magnificent *chateaux*, or castles, in the Loire Valley. These royal residences were designed and decorated by Italian artists. French artists traveled to Italy as well. Jean Fouquet, the most celebrated French painter of the fifteenth century, spent several years in Italy. The French Renaissance reached its peak, however, in the sixteenth century, during the reigns of Francis I (1515 to 1547) and his son Henry II (1547 to 1559). Francis I brought Leonardo da Vinci to France and spent huge sums of money on new construction, including his flamboyant hunting lodge, Chambord.

Above and below:
Jean Fouquet,
Etienne Chevalier
(above) and *St. Stephen* (below),
1447, panel,
Staatliche Museen,
Berlin.

✦ THE FRENCH
MONARCHY
For France, as in most of Europe, the fifteenth and sixteenth centuries were marked by wars. The Hundred Years' War (1337–1453), a protracted series of battles between France and England, ended in 1453. In 1477, King Louis XI (ruled 1461–1486) took advantage of the death of Charles the Bold, the last Duke of Burgundy, to seize the powerful Duchy of Burgundy and make it part of France. His successor, Charles VIII, invaded Italy in 1494 in hopes of gaining more territory. In 1499, Louis XII (1498–1515) seized the Duchy of Milan. Francis I (1515–1547) fought a series of battles with the Holy Roman Emperor Charles V. At the same time, he was a great patron of the arts who managed to bring a thriving culture to his warring kingdom.

THE KINGDOM OF
FRANCE AND THE
DUCHY OF
BURGUNDY

✦ THE TOWERS
The chateau itself has four massive towers. Four more were planned for the corners of the wall surrounding it, but only two were completed.

✦ CHAMBORD
Massive Chambord (right) was built as a hunting lodge for Francis I. It took longer than twenty years to build and is the largest chateau in the Loire Valley. It has more than 400 rooms and 365 fireplaces.

✦ THE COURTYARD
The courtyard was used to receive guests and also as an area for tournaments, games, and open-air spectacles.

✦ COUSIN THE ELDER
Jean Cousin the Elder (c. 1490–c. 1560) was a painter, engraver, and sculptor who also designed tapestries and stained-glass windows. His son, Jean Cousin the Younger, also became a painter. Left: Jean Cousin, *Eve as Pandora*, c. 1549, panel, 38.5 x 59 in. (98 x 150 cm), Louvre, Paris.

✦ THE ROOF
The roof, with its multitude of turrets, gables, and chimneys, is the most distinctive feature of the chateau.

✦ JEAN FOUQUET
Jean Fouquet (c. 1420–c. 1480) introduced Italian painting techniques to France. He is known for his exquisite portraits, altarpieces, and illustrated manuscripts. Above: Jean Fouquet, *Portrait of the Clown Gonnella*, before 1441, detail, tempera on panel, 14.2 x 9.5 in. (36 x 24 cm), Kunsthistorisches Museum, Vienna.

THE CANAL ✦
All the materials used to build the chateau were brought to the site on barges along a canal specially built to connect the chateau with the nearby Loire River.

SPAIN

Spain became a unified kingdom and a major world power during the Renaissance. Unification began in the fifteenth century under the Spanish sovereigns Ferdinand and Isabella. Their sponsorship of Christopher Columbus's voyage in 1492 increased Spain's wealth and influence. During the next century, riches from the New World enabled Spain to become the dominant power in Europe. While Spain expanded its empire overseas, the arts at home flourished. The sixteenth century was the age of El Greco, one of Spain's greatest painters.

Titian, *Portrait of Philip II*, 1551, oil on canvas, 76 x 43.75 in. (193 x 111 cm), Prado, Madrid.

✦ A WORLD POWER

The marriage of Isabella of Castile and Ferdinand of Aragon in 1469 led to the unification of the two largest kingdoms on the Iberian peninsula. In 1492, the two rulers conquered the kingdom of Granada, which had been a Muslim stronghold for over 700 years. That same year, Christopher Columbus landed in the Americas, an event that would bring new wealth to Spain. The unifications under Ferdinand and Isabella laid the foundation for the Kingdom of Spain, which would become a major world power in the sixteenth century. Between 1516 and 1556, Spain was ruled by Charles I, better known as Charles V, the Holy Roman Emperor. He inherited the Spanish realm upon the death of Ferdinand, who was his grandfather. During Charles's reign, the Spanish Empire expanded to include much of Central and South America and Mexico. Silver and gold from the New World financed Spanish wars in Europe, including the Spanish Armada's attempted invasion of England in 1588.

✦ SPAIN IN THE MID-FIFTEENTH CENTURY
Until unified by Ferdinand and Isabella, Spain was divided into separate kingdoms, including Castile, Navarre, Aragon, and Granada.

✦ THE CARRACK
The Spanish used the three-masted carrack to explore the world in the fifteenth and sixteenth centuries.

✦ CARGO
Barrels of oil are being loaded onto a ship. The port of Sanlúcar prepared ships for transatlantic voyages. Barges helped with loading and unloading of cargo.

♦ THE DISROBING OF CHRIST
The painting is one of El Greco's first works in Spain. He was criticized for placing Jesus's head below the figures in the background, yet the figure of Jesus, clothed in bright red, is clearly the dominant feature of the painting.
El Greco, *Disrobing of Christ*, 1577–1579, oil on canvas, 112 x 68 in. (285 x 173 cm), Cathedral, Toledo.

♦ ADORATION
El Greco, *Adoration of the Name of Jesus*, 1597, oil on canvas, Monastery of San Lorenzo, Escorial, Madrid.

Self-portrait of El Greco, detail from *The Burial of Count Orgaz*.

♦ EL GRECO
El Greco was born Domenikos Theotokopoulos on the island of Crete in 1541. Today, Crete is part of Greece, but at that time, it was part of the Venetian Republic. The artist became known as El Greco in Italy and Spain. He left Crete in 1568 for Venice, where he encountered the art of Titian. El Greco's bold colors are similar to Titian's. In 1576, El Greco left Italy for Spain and settled in Toledo. He painted an altarpiece, *The Disrobing of Christ*, for the new cathedral in Toledo. Many of El Greco's works have religious themes. He was working during the Counter-Reformation, a period in which the Catholic Church challenged the threat posed by the Protestant Reformation. Spain's Catholic rulers encouraged art that would inspire religious feelings. El Greco's style is unique, intense, and haunting. He blends elements of Renaissance art with those of the Byzantine tradition, which was still very much alive in his native Crete. His distorted figures and expressive style inspired artists of the twentieth century.

♦ PORT OF SANLÙCAR
Sanlúcar was one of the most important ports in Spain in the fifteenth and sixteenth centuries. Christopher Columbus departed on his third voyage from Sanlúcar. It was also a departure point for Magellan.

♦ WAREHOUSES AND DOCKYARDS
Merchandise passing through the port was stored in warehouses along the wharf. Dockyards handled the maintenance of boats and ships.

♦ COASTAL TRADING
Small, single-masted ships were used for coastal trading.

♦THE MIRACLE
Inspired by a Spanish legend, this is one of El Greco's most famous works. El Greco, *The Burial of Count Orgaz*, 1586–1588, oil on canvas, Church of San Tomè, Toledo.

Above: Hans Holbein the Younger, *Portrait of Nicholas Kratzer*, 1528, tempera on panel, 32.5 x 26.5 in. (83 x 67 cm), Louvre, Paris.

ENGLAND

The English Renaissance did not begin until the sixteenth century. Unlike the Italian Renaissance, which centered on the visual arts, the English Renaissance is remarkable for its literature. England produced important poets, philosophers, and playwrights. Its most famous playwright was William Shakespeare (1564–1616), a figure who has come to respresent the English Renaissance. Shakespeare produced his plays during the reign of Elizabeth I. Literature and music flourished under Elizabeth, while painting remained a minor art. Nevertheless, two painters are associated with Renaissance England: the gifted miniaturist, Nicholas Hilliard, and Henry VIII's brilliant court portrait painter, Hans Holbein.

♦ **HANS HOLBEIN THE YOUNGER**
Hans Holbein was born in Germany in 1497. He executed brilliant portraits of Henry VIII, his courtiers, and leading figures in English society. He died of plague in London in 1543. *Portrait of Henry VIII*, 1536–1537, tempera on panel, 11 x 7.5 in. (28 x 19 cm), Thyssen Collection, Lugano.

♦ **THE TUDORS**
The English Renaissance occurred during the reign of the Tudors. Henry VII was the first Tudor king of England (ruled 1485–1509). He was succeeded by Henry VIII (1509–1547), married to Catherine of Aragon. Henry asked Pope Clement VII to grant him a divorce so that he could marry Anne Boleyn. When the pope refused, Henry broke away from the Catholic Church and established the Church of England. This led to years of religious strife. After the short reigns of Henry's children Edward VI and Mary I, the crown passed to his daughter Elizabeth I, who ruled for forty-five years (1558–1603). The last Tudor monarch, her reign is known as England's Golden Age.

Below: Hans Holbein the Younger, *Thomas More*, 1527, detail, pen and ink on paper, Kunstmuseum, Basel.

♦ **THE UNIVERSITY OF OXFORD**
The oldest university in England, Oxford witnessed a renewed interest in the Greek language, mathematics, astronomy, geography, and other scientific disciplines during the Renaissance.

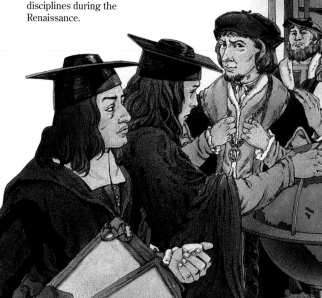

♦ **NICHOLAS HILLIARD**
The most celebrated miniature painted by Hilliard (c. 1547–1619) depicts a young lover surrounded by roses — and thorns. Nicholas Hilliard, *Young Man Leaning Against a Tree*, 1588, watercolor, 5.25 x 2.8 in. (13.5 x 7.3 cm), Victoria and Albert Museum, London.

♦ THE GLOBE
The Age of
Exploration
inspired interest
in geography.

♦ NICHOLAS KRATZER
Court astronomer to
Henry VIII, Kratzer shows
his scientific instruments
to an attentive audience.

♦ HANS HOLBEIN
The artist studies Kratzer
for a portrait he is painting.
He and Kratzer also
produced maps together.

♦ THE AUDIENCE
Teachers and
students engage in
lively debate after
each lesson.

THE ASTROLABE ♦
This instrument indicates
the position of the Sun,
Moon, planets, and stars.
Another type of astrolabe
helped sailors navigate.

♦ TIME LINE

1401	In Florence, Lorenzo Ghiberti wins the competition to design a bronze door for the Baptistry of the new Florence Cathedral.
1416	Donatello unveils his statue of *St. George* for Orsanmichele. Florentine sculpture rises to new heights in its realism.
1425	Masaccio uses linear perspective to paint the Brancacci Chapel frescoes, bringing realism to Florentine painting.
1434	Flemish painter Jan van Eyck paints his masterpiece *Giovanni Arnolfini and His Wife.*
1453	The fall of Constantinople to the Ottomans. The end of the Hundred Years' War in England leads to the rise of the Tudors.
1454	The five largest states in Italy sign a treaty, the Peace of Lodi, which establishes a forty-year period of relative peace in Italy.
1460	Piero della Francesca paints the *Flagellation* in Urbino. His work has a strong influence on the artists of central and northern Italy.
1474	Mantegna, having absorbed the achievements of Donatello and Masaccio, completes the frescoes in the Ducal Palace of Mantua.
1475	Venetian artist Giovanni Bellini meets Antonello da Messina and assimilates Flemish innovations.
1492	The discovery of the New World marks the beginning of a new era for Spain. Lorenzo the Magnificent dies in Florence.
1494	Charles VIII of France invades Italy, initiating a long series of battles known as the Italian Wars.
1497	Leonardo da Vinci finishes the *Last Supper* at Santa Maria delle Grazie in Milan.
1504	Leonardo lives and works in Florence for a brief time. He finishes *David* and makes the first studies for the *Mona Lisa.*
1508	In Rome, Michelangelo begins work on the Sistine Chapel ceiling and Raphael works on the Vatican Stanze.
1516	In Venice, Titian begins painting the *Assumption of the Virgin.* Leonardo moves to the court of the French king Francis I.
1517	The Protestant Reformation begins in Wittenburg, Germany, when Martin Luther attacks church abuses.
1534	The English Parliament recognizes Henry VIII as head of the Church of England, separated from Rome.
1550	Work is finished on Chambord, a chateau built for Francis I in the Loire Valley. It is a symbol of the French Renaissance.
1559	A peace treaty ends the Italian Wars. Italy moves into the age of the Counter-Reformation.
1577	El Greco paints *The Disrobing of Christ.* El Greco is the most important painter at the court of Philip II of Spain.

♦ GLOSSARY

allegory: a story which has a symbolic meaning and often carries a moral message

apprentice: a beginner who works with a master in order to learn a trade

bas-relief: a sculpture in which the images project slightly from a flat background

city-state: a self-governing state consisting of a main city and its surrounding territory

duchy: territory ruled by a duke or duchess

fresco: a painting on a wall, executed while the plaster is wet

guild: an organization of people in the same trade or business

Iberian peninsula: the peninsula that includes modern-day Spain and Portugal

mercenary: a professional soldier who is hired and paid to fight

Ottoman Empire: a vast, Turkish-ruled state, founded in 1299, that lasted until 1922

pigment: a dry substance, usually pulverized, that gives paint its color

translucent: clear; allowing light to pass

triptych: an artwork consisting of three panels joined by hinges

WEB SITES

The Medici and the Italian Renaissance
www.pbs.org/empires/medici/renaissance/index.html
A wealth of information on the Italian Renaissance, including photographs and an interactive time line and tour of Florence.

The Renaissance
www.learner.org/exhibits/renaissance
A comprehensive guide to the Renaissance, including art, science, trade, and exploration.

The Florence Cathedral
www.duomofirenze.it/storia/storia_eng.htm
Tour a Renaissance masterpiece.

♦ LIST OF WORKS INCLUDED IN THIS BOOK

The works reproduced in this book are listed below, with their date, when known, the museum or gallery where they are currently held, and the number of the page on which they appear. Where no gallery is shown, the work is in a private collection. The numbers in bold type refer to the credits on page 64, which give further information about some of the works. The works are listed in alphabetical order by the artist.
Abbreviations:
E = entire; D = detail

Abbreviations: APM, Alte Pinakothek, Munich; BM, Brera, Milan; BW, Bargello Museum, Florence; KMW, Kunsthistorisches Museum, Vienna; NGL, National Gallery, London; VR, Vatican, Rome.

ANONYMOUS
1. *Belvedere Apollo*, 2nd century A.D., marble (VR) 9 E; **2.** Cameo with portrait of Ludovico il Moro (Museo degli Argenti, Florence) 27 E; 3. *Emperor Claudius*, first half of the 1st century AD., marble (VR) 30 E; 4. *Ideal City*, late 15th century, tempera on panel, 67.5 x 239 cm. (Galleria Nazionale delle Marche, Urbino) 21 E; 5. Laocoön, 1st century A.D., marble (Cortile del Belvedere, VR) 30 E; 6. *Rabbit-Hunting with a Ferret*, c. 1560, tapestry, 300 x 360 cm. (M.H. De Young Memorial Museum, San Francisco) 42 D; **7.** *Section of the dome of Florence Cathedral*, c. 1440, drawing 10 E; **8.** *The Nile*, Hellenistic statue, marble (Cortile del Belvedere, VR) 30 E; **9.** *Venus Felix*, marble (Cortile Ottagono, VR) 31 E; **10.** *View of Rome After the Building of Sixtus V in 1602*, engraving (Raccolta Stampe Archivio Bertarelli, Milan) 30-31 E
ALTDORFER, ALBRECHT
11. *Crucifixion*, c.1520, oil on gold base on panel, 75 x 57.5 cm. (Museum of Art Budapest) 54 E
ANDREA DEL CASTAGNO
12. *Last Supper*, 1447, fresco, 470 x 975 cm. (Convent of Sant'Apollonia, Florence) 17 E
ANGELICO, FRA
13. *Annunciation*, c.1438, fresco, 230 x 321 cm. (Monastery of San Marco, Florence) 16 E;**14.** *St. Dominic at the Foot of the Cross*, 1442, fresco, 237 x 125 cm. (Monastery of San Marco, Florence) 16 E
ANTONELLO DA MESSINA
15. *Annunciation*, 1475, oil on panel, 45 x. 34.5 em. (Galleria Nazionale, Palermo) 37 F; **16.** *Condottiere*, 1475, oil on panel, 35 x 28 cm. (Louvre, Paris) 39 E; **17.** *Self-portrait*, 1473, oil on panel, 35.5 x 25.5 cm. (NGL) 37 E
BELLINI, GENTILE
18. *Procession in St. Mark's Square*, 1496, oil on canvas, 367 x 745 cm. (Accademia, Venice) 39 E
BELLINI, GIOVANNI
19. *Dead Christ Supported by Mary and St. John the Evangelist* (Pieta), c.1467, tempera on panel, 86 x 107 cm. (BM) 38 E, D; **20.** *Dead Christ Supported by Two Angels* (Pieta), c. 1452, panel, 74 x 50 cm. (Correr Museum, Venice) 38 E; **21.** *Greek Madonna*, c.1475, tempera on panel, 84 x 62 cm. (BM) 38 E; **22.** *Madonna and Child*, 1508, oil on canvas, 85 x 115 cm. (BM), 39 E; **23.** *Polyptych of St. Vincent Ferrer*, before 1464, panel (Church of SS Giovanni e Paolo, Venice) 38 E; **24.** *Portrait of a Man*, 1480-90, panel, 32.8 x 25.5 cm. (Louvre, Paris) 39 E; **25.** Portrait of Doge Loredan, c.1501, oil on panel, 62 x 45 cm. (NGL) 36 E; **26.** *San Giobbe altarpiece*, c.1478, panel, 471 x 258 em. (Accadernia, Venice) 39 E, D
BEMBO, BONIFACIO
27. *Portrait of Bianca Maria Sforza*, 1460, tempera on canvas, 49 x 31 cm. (BM) 26 E; **28.** *Portrait of Francesco Sforza*, 1460, tempera on canvas, 49 x 31 cm. (BM) 26 E
BOSCH, HIERONYMUS
29. *Prodigal Son*, c.1510, oil on canvas, diameter 70.6 cm. (Boymans-van Betmingen Museum, Rotterdam) 45 E
BOTTICELLI, SANDRO
30. *Birth of Venus*, c. 1483-85, tempera on canvas, 172 x 278 cm. Uffizi, Florence) 17 E
BRUEGEL, PIETER THE ELDER
31. *Children's Games*, 15W, oil on panel, 118 x 161 cm. (KMV) 48 E, D, 49 D; **32.** *Peasant Wedding*, c.1568, oil on panel, 114 x 163 cm.) 49 E, D; **33.** *Self-portrait*, c.1565, drawing in pen and brown ink, 25 x 21.6 cm. (Albertina, Vienna) 48 D; **34.** *The Land of Cockaigne*, 1567, oil on panel, 52 x 72- cm. (APM) 49 E
BRUNELLESCHI, FILIPPO
35. *Sacrifice of Isaac*, panel for a door of Florence Baptistry, 1401, bronze relief (BMF) 12 E
CAMPIN, ROGER
36. *St. Veronica*, c.1430, tempera on panel, 144 x 53 cm. (Stadelscher Kunstinstitut, Frankfurt) 45 D; 37. *Virgin and Child Before a Firescreen*, 1420-25, tempera on panel 63 x 48 cm. (NGL) 44 E
CARPACCIO, VITTORE
38. *Arrival of the Ambassadors of Britain at the Court of Brittany*, from the Stories of St. Ursula, 1490-96, tempera on panel, 275 x 589 cm. (Accademia, Venice) 7 E
COUSIN, JEAN THE ELDER
39. *Eve as Pandora*, c.1549, panel, 98 x 150 cm. (Louvre, Paris) 57 E
CRANACH, LUCAS THE ELDER
40. *Albrecht of Brandenburg Before the Crucifixion*, 1520-25, panel, 158 x 112 cm. (APM) 54 E
DOMENICO VENEZIANO
41. *Annunciation, from the St. Lucy altarpiece*, 1445-47, tempera on panel, 27.3 x 54 cm. (Fitzwilliam Museum, Cambridge, England) 18 E; **42.** *Madonna and Child with St. Francis, St. John the Baptist, St. Zenobius and St. Lucy*, from the St. Lucy altar piece, 1445-47, tempera on panel, 209 x 216 cm. (Uffizi, Florence) 18 E, D; **43.** *Martyrdom of St. Lucy*, from the St. Lucy altarpiece, 1445-47, tempera on panel, 25 x 28.5 cm. (Gemaldegalerie, Berlin) 18 E; **44.** *Miracle of St. Zenobius*, from the St. Lacy altarpiece, 1445-47, tempera on panel, 28.6 x 32.5 em. (Fitzwilliam Museum, Cambridge, England) 18 E; **45.** *St. Francis Receives the Stigmata*, from the St. Lucy altarpiece, 1445-47, tempera on panel, 26.7 x 30.5 cm. (National Gallery of Art, Washington, DC) 18 E; **46.** *St. John the Baptist in the Desert*, from the St. Lucy altarpiece, 1445-47, tempera on panel, 28.3 x 32.4 cm. (National Gallery of Art, Washington, DC) 18 E
DONATELLO (DONATO DI NICOLO DI BETTO BARDI)
47. *Feast of Herod*, 1427, bronze relief (Church of San Giovanni, Siena) 13 E; **48.** *St. George*, 1415-16, marble, height 378 cm. (BMF) 12 E, D
DÜRER, ALBRECHT
49. *Adam*, 1507, oil on panel, 209 x 81 cm. (Prado, Madrid) 54 E; **50.** *Adoration of the Magi*, 1504, oil on panel, 100 x 114 em. (Uffizi, Florence) 54 E, D; **51.** *Eve*, 1507, oil on panel, 209 x 83 cm. (Prado, Madrid) 54 E; **52.** *Four Apostles*, 1526, oil on panel, 215.5 x 76 cm. (APM) 54 E; **53.** *Nativity*, 1504, oil on panel, 155 x 126 cm. (APM) 55 E; **54.** *Self-portrait*, 1500, oil on panel, 67 x 49 cm. (AM) 55 E; **55.** *The Emperor Maximilian 1*, 1519, oil on panel, 74 x 61.5 cm. (KMV) 50 E
ERHART, MICHEL
56. *St. John the Evangelist*, c.1493, wood sculpture (Monastery Church, Blaubeuren) 53 D
EYCK, HUBERT AND JAN VAN
57. *The Adoration of the Lamb*, 1420-32, oil on panel, 137.7 x 242.3 cm. (Cathedral of St. Bavon, Ghent) 44 E, D
EYCK, JAN VAN
58. *Giovanni Arnolfini and his Wife*, 1434, oil on panel, 82 x 60 cm. (NGL) 45 E, D; **59.** *Man in a Turban*, 1433, oil on panel, 25.5 x 19 CM. (NGL) 46 E; **60.** *Portrait of Margaret van Eyck*, 1439, oil on panel, 41.2 x 34.6 cm. (Groeningemuseum, Bruges) 45 D; **61.** *The Madonna of Chancellor Rolin*, c.1434, oil on panel, 66 x 62 cm. (Louvre, Paris) 47 E, D
FOUQUET, JEAN
62. *Etienne Chevalier and St. Stephen*, 1447, tempera on panel, 95 x 85 cm. (Staatliche Museen, Berlin) 56 D; **63.** *Portrait of the Clown Gonnella*, before 1441, tempera on panel, 36 x 24 cm. (KMV) 57 E
GHIBERTI, LORENZO
64. *Sacrifice of Isaac*, panel for a door of Florence Baptistry, 1401, bronze relief (BMF) 12 E; **65.** *St. John the Baptist*, 1412-16, bronze, height 254 cm. (Orsanmichele, Florence) 13 E; **66.** *St. Matthew*, 1419-22, bronze, height 270 cm. (Orsanmichele, Florence) 13 E, D
GHIRLANDAIO (DOMENICO BIGORDI)
67. *Angel Appearing to Zacharias*, 1490, fresco, 250 x 450 cm. (Tornabuoni Chapel, Santa Maria Novella, Florence) 9 D; **68.** *Miracle of the French Notary's Child*, 1480, fresco (Sassetti Chapel, Santa Trinita, Florence) 17 E
GIORGIONE
69. *Enthroned Madonna and Child*, 1504-5, panel, 200 x 152 cm. (San Liberale, Castelfranco Veneto) 40 E; **70.** *The Tempest*, c. 1506, oil on canvas, 82 x 73 cm. (Accademia, Venice) 40 E, D; **71.** *The Three Philosophers*, 1508, oil on canvas, 123.5 x 144.5 cm. (KNV) 40 D
GRECO, EL
72. *Adoration of the Name of Jesus*, 1597, oil on canvas, 140 x 110 cm. (Monastery of San Lorenzo, Escorial, Madrid) 59 E; **73.** *Disrobing of Christ*, 1577-79, oil on canvas, 285 x 173 cm. (Cathedral, Toledo) 59 E; **74.** *The Burial of Count Orgaz*, 1586-88, oil on canvas, 140 x 340 cm. (Church of San Tome, Toledo) 59 E, D
GRÜNEWALD, MATHIAS
75. *Crucifixion with Sts. Anthony and Sebastian*, 1512-16, oil on panel, central panel 269 x 307 cm., side panels 237 x 76 em. (Unterlinden Museum, Colmar) 55 E, D
HILLIARD, NICHOLAS
76. *Young Man Leaning Against a Tree*, 1588, watercolor, 13.5. x 7.3 cm. (Victoria and Albert Museum, London) 60 E
HOLBEIN, HANS THE YOUNGER
77. *Portrait of Erasmus of Rotterdam*, 1523, tempera on panel, 43 x 33 cm. (Louvre, Paris) 55 E; **78.** *Portrait of Henry VIII*, 1536-37, tempera on panel, 28 x 19 cm. Thyssen Collection, Lugano) 60 E; **79.** *Portrait of Nicholas Kratzer*, 1528, tempera on panel, 83 x 67 cm. (Louvre, Paris) 60 E; **80.** *The Ambassadors*, 1533, tempera on panel, 207 x 209 cm. (NGL) 7 E; **81.** *Thomas More*, 1527, pen and ink on paper, 38.7 x 52.4 cm. (Kunstmuseum, Basel) 60 D
LEONARDO DA VINCI
82. *Mona Lisa*, 1505-14, oil on panel, 77 x 53 em. (Louvre, Paris) 28 E, 29 D; **83.** *The Last Supper*, 1495-97, tempera on wall, 460 x 880 cm. (Refectory, Santa Maria delle Grazie, Milan) 26 E
LIPPI, FILIPPINO
84. *Adoration of the Magi*, 1496, oil on panel, 258 x 243 cm. (Uffizi, Florence) 16 E
LIPPI, FILIPPO
85. *Madonna and Child with the Birth of the Virgin*, 1452, panel, diameter 135 cm. (Pitti Palace, Florence) 16 E
MANTEGNA ANDREA
86. Camera Picta, 1465-74, frescoes (Ducal Palace, Mantua) 25 D
MASACCIO (TOMMASO DI SER GIOVANNI DI MONE CASSAI)
87. *Expulsion*, 1425, fresco, 214 x 90 cm. (Brancacci Chapel, Santa Maria del Carmine, Florence) 14 E; **88.** *St. Peter Baptizing the Neophytes*, 1425, fresco, 24.7 x 172 cm. (Brancacci Chapel, Santa Maria del Carmine, Florence) 15 E, D; **89.** *St. Peter Healing with His Shadow*, 1426-27, fresco, 232 x 162 cm. (Brancacci Chapel, Santa Maria del Carmine, Florence) 15 E, D; **90.** *The Distribution of the Goods of the Community and the Death of Ananias*, 1426-27, fresco, 232 x 157 cm. (Brancacci Chapel, Santa Maria del Carmine, Florence) 15 E, D; **91.** *The Raising of the Son of Theophilus*, 1427-28, fresco, 230 x 598 cm. (Brancacci Chapel, Santa Maria del Carmine, Florence) 14 D
92. *The Tribute Money*, 1425, fresco, 247 x 597 cm. (Brancacci Chapel, Santa Maria del Carmine, Florenope) 14 E, D; 93. 71e Trinity, 1426-28, fresco, 640 x 317 cm. (Santa Maria di Novella, Florence) 14 E
MEMLING, HANS
94. *Arrival of St. Utsula in Cologne*, detail of the *Reliquary of St. Ursula*, 1489, oil on panel, 87 x 91 x 33 cm. (Hans Memling Museum, Bruges) 45 D
MICHELANGELO BUONARROTTI
95. *David*, 1501-4, marble, height 410 cm. (Accademia, Florence) 28 E, 29 D; **96.** *Delphic Sibyl*, 1511, fresco, 395 x 380 cm. (Sistine Chapel, VR) 32 E; **97.** *Libyan Sibyl*, 1511, fresco, 395 x 380 cm. (Sistine Chapel, VR) 32 E; **98.** *Moses*, 1515, marble, height 235 cm. (San Pietro in Vincoli, Rome) 32 E; **99.** *Prophets of the Sistine Chapel*, 1511, fresco (Sistine Chapel, vR) 32 E, 33 E; **100.** *Tomb of Julius* 11, 1515, marble (San Pietro in Vincoli, Rome) 32 E
NANNI DI BANCO, ANTONIO
101. *Four Crowned Martyrs*, c.1410-12, marble, life-size (Orsanmichele, Florence) 13 E
PIERO DELLA FRANCESCA
102. *Annunciation*, c.1470, oil and tempera on panel, 122 x 194 cm. (Galleria Nazionale dell'Umbria, Perugia) 11 D; **103.** *Baptism of Christ*, 1448-54, tempera on panel, 167 x 116 cm. (NGL) 19 E, D; **104.** *Flagellation*, c.1460, oil and tempera on panel, 59 x 81.5 cm. (Galleria Nazionale delle Marche, Urbino) 20 E, D; **105.** *Madonna and Cltild with Saints*, 1472-74, oil and panel, 248 x 170 cm. (Bm) 19 E; **106.** *Montefeltro Diptych, Portrait of Battista Sforza, Portrait of Federico da Montefeltro*, 1465, oil on panel, 47 x 33 cm. (Uffizi, Florence) 20 E
POLLAIOLO ANTONIO
107. *St. Sebastian*, 1475, tempera on panel, 292 x 203 cm. (NGL) 17 E
PONTORNO JACOPO
108. *Cosimo the Elder*, c.1518, oil on panel, 86 x 65 cm. (Uffizi, Florence) 10 D
RAPHAEL
109. *Disputation- over the Sacrament*, c.1509, fresco, base 770 cm. (VR) 34 E; **110.** *Galatea*, 1511, fresco, 295 x 225 cm. (Villa Farnesina, Rome) 31 E; **111.** *Liberation of St. Peter from Prison*, 1513, fresco, base 660 cm. (VR) 35 E; **112.** *Madonna of the Goldfinch*, 1507, oil on panel, 107 x 77 cm. (Uffizi, Florence) 34 E; **113.** *Portrait of Angelo Doni*, c.1506, oil on panel, 63 x 45 cm. (Pitti Palace, Florence) 28 E, 29 D; **114.** *Portrait of Leo X*, 1516-19, tempera on panel, 154 x 119 cm. (Uffizi, Florence) 30 D; **115.** *Self-portrait*, 1506, oil on panel, 43 x 53 cm. (Uffizi, Florence) 34 E; **116.** *The School of Athens*, c.1510, fresco, base 770 cm. (VR) 6 D; 34 E, D, 35 D
STOSS VEIT
117. *High Altar*, 1520-23, wood sculpture, carpentry in firwood, carving in limewood, height 355 cm. (Cathedral, Barnberg) 53 E, D
TITIAN
118. *Assumption of the Virgin*, 1516-18, oil on panel, 690 x 360 cm. (Church of Santa Maria Gloriosa dei Frari, Venice) 41 E; **119.** *Charles V on Horseback*, 1548, oil on canvas, 332 x 279 cm. (Prado, Madrid) 41 E; **120.** *Danae*, 1553-54, oil on canvas, 128 x 178 cm. (Prado, Madrid) 41 E; **121.** *Pope Paul III with Alessandro and Ottavio Farnese*, 1546, oil. on canvas, 210 x 174 cm. (Capodimonte Gallery, Naples) 41 E; **122.** *Portrait of Philip 11*, 1551, oil on canvas, 193 x 111 cm. (Prado, Madrid) 58 E; **123.** *Self-portrait*, 1565-70, oil on canvas, 86 x 65 cm. (Prado, Madrid) 41 E
TURA, COSIMO
124. *Madonna Enthroned with Musician Angels*, c.1480, oil on panel, 239 x 101 cm. (NGL) 22 D, 23 E; **125.** *Spring*, c.1460, oil on panel, 116.2 x 101 cm. (NGL) 23 E
UCCELLO, PAOLO (PAOLO DI DONO)
126. Battle of San Romano, 1456, tempera on panel, 182 x 317 cm. (NGL) 7 E; **127.** *Miracle of the Host*, 1465-69, tempera on panel, 43 x 351 cm. (Galleria Nazionale delle Marche, Urbino) 19 D
VERROCCHIO (ANDREA DI FRANCESCO DI CIONE)
128. *Head of St. Jerome*, c.1460, tempera on paper glued on panel, 49 x 46 cm. (Pitti Palace, Florence) 16 D
WEYDEN, ROGIER VAN DER
129. *Descent from the Cross*, c. 1435, oil on panel, 220 x 262 cm (Prado, Madrid) 45 E

◆ INDEX

◆ CREDITS

The original and previously unpublished illustrations in this book were created at the request of, and by, DoGi s.rl., who holds the copyright.

ILLUSTRATIONS: Simone Boni (50-51,60-61); Lorenzo Cecchi (20-21,36-37, 58-59); Boni-Cecchi (56-57); L.R. Galante (4-5, 6-7, 8-9, 24-25, 52-53); L.R. Galante-Manuela Cappon (42-43, 46-47); L.R. Galante-Francesco Petracchi (10-11, 22-23, 26-27)
Maps: Luca Cascioli (7 r, 8 c, 20 r, 42 c, 51 b, 56 r, 58 r)
Views: Lorenzo Cecchi and Francesco Petracchi: 11 r, 23 l, 36 c
COVER: L R Galante
BACK COVER: L. R. Galante
FRONTISPIECE: L. R. Galante-Manuela Cappon

REPRODUCTIONS OF ARTISTS' WORKS
ALTE PINAKOTHEK, MUNICH: 40,52,54; ARCHIVIO ALINARI, FLORENCE: 22,85,106, 113,114,127; ARCHIVIO ALINARI,FLORENCE/GIRAUDON, FLORENCE, PARIS: 18,19,26,38,57, 73,,74,79,120,122,123,129; ARCHIVIO ALINARI,/GIRAUDON/LAUROS, FLORENCE, PARIS:

15,16,39,61; ARCHIVIO. DOGI, FIRENZE: 7,12,20,47,48,56.58,64,65, 66,69,83,84,98,100,126,110,117,121; ARCHIVIO DOGI (FOTO SAPORETTI): 10; ARCHIVIO DOGI (QUATTRONE).: 13, 14, 35, 42, 67, 68, 86, 87, 88, 89, 90, 91, 92, 93, 95, 101, 112, 115, 128; ARCHIVIO SCALA, FLORENCE: 23, 34, 72, 82, 111; BOYMANS-VAN BEUNINGEN MUSEUM, ROTTERDAM: 29; BRERA, MILAN: 28, 105; THE BRIDGEMAN ART LIBRARY, LONDON: 4, 11, 21, 25,27,30,31, 32,41, 53, 70, 75, 76, 80, 104, 109, 118; ERIC LESSING, VIENNA: 24, 33, 63, 78; FITZWILLIAM- MUSEUM, CAMBRIDGE, ENGLAND: 44; GALLERIA NAZIONALE DELL'UMBRIA, PERUGIA: 102; GEMÄLDEGALERIE, BERLIN: 43; GROENINGEMUSEUM, BRUGES: 60; HANS MEMLING, MUSEUM, BRUGES: 94; JORG P ANDERS PHOTO, BERLIN: 62; KUNSTHISTORISCHE MUSEUM, VIENNA: 55, 71, KUNSTMUSUM, BASEL,: 81; M.H.DEYOUNG MEMORIAL MUSEUM, SAN FRANCISCO: 6; MUSEO DEGLI ARGENTI FLORENCE: 2; NATIONAL GALLERY, LONDON: 17, 37, 59, 103, 107, 124. 125; NATIONAL GALLERY OF ART, WASHINGTON: 45, 46; PRADO, MADRID: 49, 51, 119; RMN, PARIS: 77; STÄDELSCHER KUNSTINSTITUT FRANKFURT: 36; THYSSEN COLLECTION, LUGANO 77; UFFIZI, FLORENCE: 50, 108; VATICAN, ROME : 1, 3, 5, 8, 9, 96, 97, 99, 116. COVER (clockwise, from top left): ARCHIVIO ALINARI: a, f, m, P, r, ARCHIVIO ALINARI /GIRAUDON: b; ARCHIVIO ALINARI /GIRAUDON / LAUROS h, q;ARCHIVIO DOGI: g, k, t, tr, ARCHIVIO DOGI (QUATTRONE): j, u, w, x; THE BRIDGEMAN ART LIBRARY d, e, i, n, o; ERIC

LESSING: l; NATIONAL GALLERY, LONDON: c, s.
BACK COVER: ARCHIVIO DOGI, FLORENCE; MUSEO DEGLI ARGENTI, FLORENCE

DOCUMENTS
Abbreviations: a - above, h - below, c - center, r - right, 1 - left.
ARCHIVIO DOGI: 10 all, b; 11 ar, 24 al, bl, ar; 30 al, c, ar, br; 31, al, ar, bl, br, c; ARCHIVIO DOGI (Marco Rabatti): 21 ar, br, ARCHIVIO DOGI (Paolo Soriani): 30 bl.

DoGi s.rl. has made every effort to trace other possible copyright holders. If any omissions or errors have been made, this will be corrected at reprint.

To Taylor, Jordyn, and
Maddox,

Dream, read, and explore!

Ryan
San Angelo
5/8/11

Sean Boyle
May 8, 2011

Bye Bye Balloon

by Ryan SanAngelo * Paintings by Sean Boyce

LiTTLe KiNG PReSS
Fairfield, CT

This book is dedicated to my mother and father for always encouraging me to "be a leader, not a follower" and to always pursue my dreams. - Ryan SanAngelo

To my mother, Ursula. - Sean Boyce

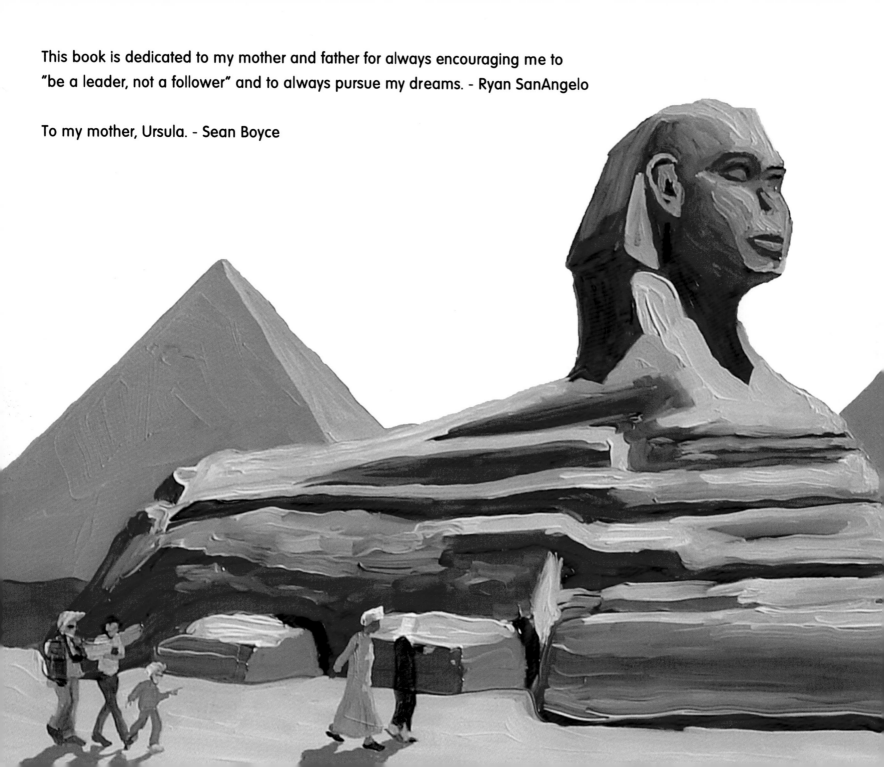

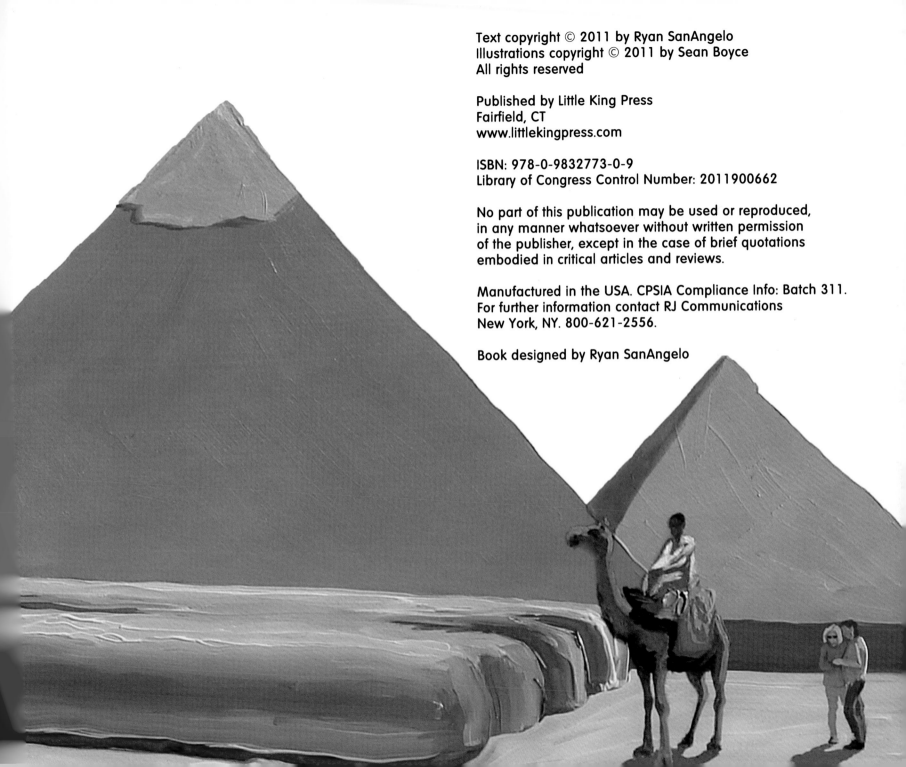

Published by Little King Press
Fairfield, CT
www.littlekingpress.com

ISBN: 978-0-9832773-0-9
Library of Congress Control Number: 2011900662

Manufactured in the USA. CPSIA Compliance Info: Batch 311.
For further information contact RJ Communications
New York, NY. 800-621-2556.

Book designed by Ryan SanAngelo

One summer Sunday, a cluster of balloons bobbed, waiting to be sold at a carnival.

Suddenly, without a sound, a blue balloon slipped free and flew into the sky.

Forward it floated towards the Statue of Liberty in New York harbor,

And coasted over the Atlantic Ocean.

It breezed by Big Ben in London, England,

And sailed past the Eiffel Tower in Paris, France.

The balloon soared above Spain, as running bulls and excitement filled the streets below.

It towered over the Leaning Tower of Pisa in Italy,

And befriended a flock of geese
above the Parthenon in Greece.

In Egypt, the balloon passed over the pyramids and Great Sphinx,

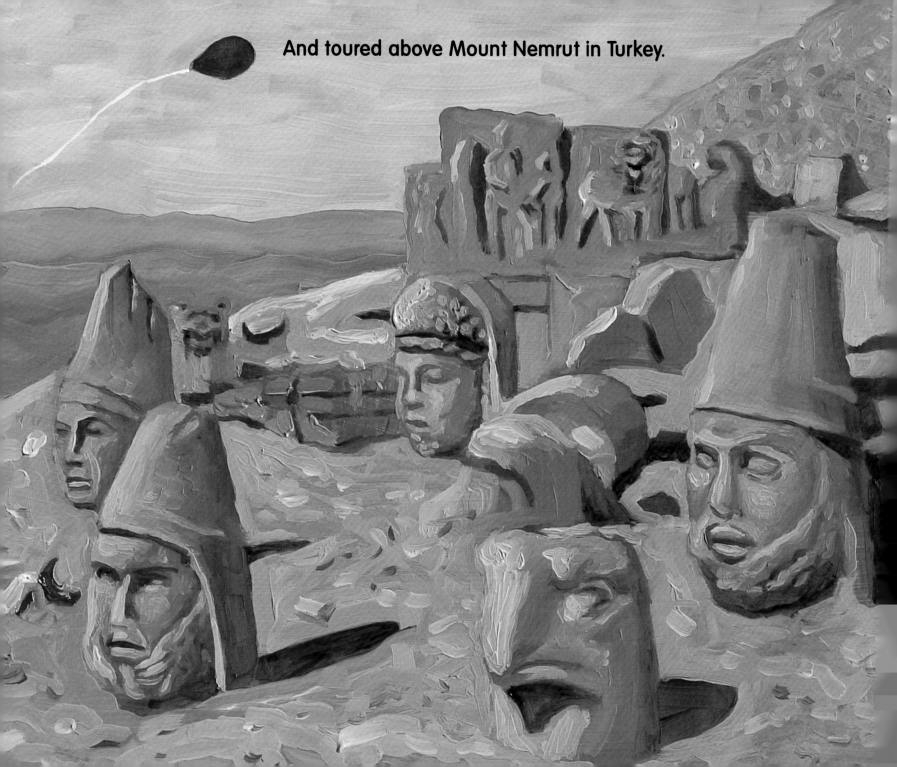

And toured above Mount Nemrut in Turkey.

It traveled over the Taj Mahal in India.

Then it glided over the Great Wall of China for miles and miles and miles.

The balloon battled wind over the Great Buddha in Japan,

But calmly cruised above kangaroos and koala bears in Australia.

It eased by Easter Island, near Chile,

And hovered above a Hollywood movie set.

Over Toronto, Canada,
the balloon grew very tired.
Losing air, it headed down.

"Look!" A boy shouted. He sprinted to catch the balloon before it hit the ground.

As he held it in his hands, he looked up at the sky.
"I wonder how it got here!" his sister exclaimed.

Meanwhile, many miles away, a cluster of balloons bobbed waiting to be sold at a carnival.

Suddenly, without a sound,
a green balloon slipped free
and flew into the sky.

Bye Bye Balloon (song)

Words and music written by Ryan SanAngelo

(verse 1)
I'm a balloon and I am blue
Being like the others I cannot do
With places to go and people to see
The only way to do it, I've got to be free
So I pull and wiggle, from strength I muster
And break away from the balloon cluster
Up to the sky I rise and rise
Away I go flying so high
And you'll say

(chorus)
Bye bye, bye bye balloon
I'll see you, I'll see you soon
Bye bye, bye bye balloon

(verse 2)
Lady Liberty, Atlantic Ocean
London, Paris, I keep on coasting
To Spain, Italy, and off to Greece
The pyramids in Egypt right below me
Mount Nemrut, the Taj Mahal
All across China I follow the wall
To Japan, Australia, and Easter Island
Over Hollywood I keep on gliding
And you'll say

(chorus)
Bye bye, bye bye balloon
I'll see you, I'll see you soon
Bye bye, bye bye balloon

(verse 3)
Free, free
Free, free, free
Free is the way I want to be
Free, free
Free, free, free
To go anywhere I want to be
I'm over the people, I'm over the trees
I'm over the land and the mighty seas
I'm looking down at all the sights
These manmade creations are looking all right
I love, I love this world
Yeah I love, I love this world
With its sun and luminous moon
Bye bye
Bye bye balloon

About the author

Ryan SanAngelo writes stories and songs for children.
He is the author of *Spaghetti Eddie.* He loves music
and he loves to laugh. He lives in Fairfield, CT with
his wife Elizabeth. Visit him online at www.ryansanangelo.com.

Ryan SanAngelo   Sean Boyce

Photo by Elizabeth Chatel

About the illustrator

Sean Boyce is a Boston artist with three children.
He loves to read, paint, play, and write. To see more of his
paintings, please visit www.seanboyceart.com.